How To REALLY LOVE Your Wife

Dean Merrill

ZONDERVAN
PUBLISHING HOUSE OF THE ZONDERVAN CORPORATION
GRAND RAPIDS, MICHIGAN 49506

How to Really Love Your Wife

Formerly published as *The Husband Book*

© 1977 by The Zondervan Corporation
Grand Rapids, Michigan

This printing 1980

Library of Congress Cataloging in Publication Data

Merrill, Dean.
    The Husband Book.

    1. Husbands.   I. Title.
HQ756.M47   301.42'72'041   77-22826

ISBN 0-310-35321-1

Printed in the United States of America

Contents

1   Husbanding Is Not a Natural Talent   *9*

2   Leading by Enabling   *23*

3   People Who Need People   *37*

4   The Dance of the Dollars   *53*

5   A Master, a Mistress, and Two Slaves   *75*

6   It's a Job   *87*

7   The Household of Faith   *105*

8   What's a Christian Home?   *117*

9   Beyond Anatomy   *131*

10   Take It Easy   *149*

11   Sickness (What a Pain)   *163*

12   The Rest of the Clan   *175*

13   The Big Picture   *189*

1

Husbanding
Is Not a
Natural Talent

1

Husbanding
Is Not a
Natural Talent

If you're a carpenter, you haven't forgotten your five long years of apprenticeship.

If you're an attorney, you'll always remember the rigors of law school.

If you're a salesman, you recall the break-in period (all the mistakes you made), and you're still taking time for periodic seminars and training sessions on sales techniques.

If you're a minister, hardly a week goes by without you telling (or retelling) someone a story about your seminary days.

Some of us have spent four — or five, or six, or seven — long years in colleges and graduate schools, getting ready to make a living. Others of us have learned on the job as we've watched, questioned, and imitated a master craftsman of our trade. Some of us are still going to night school, qualifying for the next promotion, honing our skills, learning a better way to lock up that year-end bonus.

We have a second job. Its hours are more irregular, and it pays in a wide range of intangibles rather than cash. Nevertheless, it carries a good deal of responsibility and a lot of challenge. We can succeed at it, we can do a mediocre job, or we can fail. In fact, we can fail so badly that we lose the job and all it means to us.

It's called husbanding. Being the head of our house.

Who trained us for this job?

Most of us have to answer, "No one" — and that's a tragedy. It's not our fault. It's just the way things have worked out. We've been so busy learning how to read profit margin reports and how to rebuild carburetors that we've had no time to study husbanding. And even if we'd asked, there was no one to teach us.

Who ever heard of a college course on how to be a successful household head?

There have been scores of seminars and books on marriage and family life in general, and scores more on parenting — but let's face it: far too many of us have brushed these aside as basically feminine. We've told ourselves, *Yeah, that's good stuff — my wife really needs to keep up on all that.*

We've never really taken a direct look at *our* job from *our* perspective.

What we have done is plunge right on into marriage regardless. We signed up for the job the night we proposed, amid restaurant candlelight or lakeside moonlight or wherever. We said, "I'd like to take on the responsibility of being a husband." (We phrased it a bit more romantically, of course, but the meaning was the same.)

And our sweethearts responded: "Okay, you're hired." (Again, the verbiage was generally altered to fit the occasion.)

We reported for work some months later, with considerable pomp and ceremony in front of a minister and all that. Since then, we've been on the job, for better or for worse. Still no training. Still not much thought about role and responsibility. In the years since the wedding, we've plunged along doing what comes naturally, or what we and our wives have discovered by accident. Sort of like learning to swim Marine-style. We've jumped in the deep water and tried to survive.

It's not our fault that we've made such a haphazard start. It's not our fault that the culture has commonly assumed we know what we're doing. It's just the way things have turned out.

This book is an attempt to help you think about your job as the head of your household. It is, quite simply, a husband's job description.

So far, so good?

Come to think of it — how *have* we survived so far? What accounts for the way we have husbanded up to this point?

More than any of us realize, we have imitated our own fathers. If your dad took out the garbage when you were a kid, you're probably doing it now. If he refused to do it, you've probably done the same. If your dad wrote the checks and watchdogged the money in your home, you're probably doing it too. If your dad said "I love you" to your mother more than once a month, you're probably behaving similarly. (Even though as a kid you weren't within earshot of most of your father's intimate comments, you still picked up his general tone of affection or aloofness and are probably reflecting the same.)

Take the following quiz to see just how closely you're following your father's model.

	Yes	No	Yes	No
make time for frequent adult-level communication with his wife?	☐	☐	☐	☐
have a joint checking account?	☐	☐	☐	☐
object to his wife working outside the home?	☐	☐	☐	☐
miss church more than five Sundays in a year?	☐	☐	☐	☐
pray alone with any frequency?	☐	☐	☐	☐
cope well when his wife was pregnant?	☐	☐	☐	☐
change diapers?	☐	☐	☐	☐
play table games with his wife and kids?	☐	☐	☐	☐
become frustrated when his wife got sick?	☐	☐	☐	☐
get along with his in-laws?	☐	☐	☐	☐
plan vacations?	☐	☐	☐	☐

How parallel are your answers?

It's not surprising that you are in many ways a chip off the old block. After all, you started life with his genes. You are biologically similar to him. None of us know how profound and far-reaching are the influences of fundamental heredity.

And you spent the first eighteen or so years of your life — the most impressionable years — watching him.

It would be highly unusual if you *didn't* copy him — subconsciously — in the many details and decisions of being a husband. The points where the two of you differ are probably points about which you've thought a great deal and made a decision *not* to do things like your dad.

Model No. 1

Many of us have grown up under one of two rather unfortunate models. The more common in recent years is *the Abdicator*. His name is on the mailbox, and he is the legal head-of-household, but on a day-to-day basis he serves one — and only one — major purpose: to bring home a paycheck. Every Friday he walks in with the cash necessary to keep things afloat for another week, and having done so, he has pretty well made his contribution.

Did you ever wonder why a husband is commonly called a *breadwinner?* It says something about our priorities.

The rest of the time he spends like any other warm body under the same roof — eating, sleeping, reading, watching TV, and doing whatever he enjoys doing in his spare time. He's not mad at anyone (unless they get in his way); he hasn't resigned from the family. He is indeed one of the bunch. Having financed the enterprise, he now sees it as his right to enjoy the heat, electricity, and refrigerator along with everyone else.

Who is the actual head of this household? Who's in charge?

There are two possible answers:

(1) *The wife*. In many cases, she is the real manager. Once the financial wheels have been greased, she can take it from there. She controls the buying of groceries, clothing, and furniture. She decides the menus and when the family will eat out. She administers discipline to the children, settles arguments, participates in the PTA, and makes sure everyone sees the dentist on time. She sets the spiritual tone of the household as well as how often church is attended. Having worked this hard, she is in a good position to control what happens in the bedroom as well, unless she chooses to surrender this right in exchange for the continued domination of everything else. She is the power behind the throne, the neck that turns the figurehead.

(2) The other possibility, somewhat less frequent, is that *nobody* is in control of the household. A few basic jobs may have been passed out, but beyond that, it's every person for himself. Fix your own meals when you like, go where you want, stay out of trouble, help the other person if it's to your advantage to do so, but otherwise forget it. Laissez faire is the rule.

This is actually more of a hotel than a home. People come and go as they please, encountering one another only by chance and contributing to one another only the minimum necessary to prevent anarchy.

Model No. 2

The second unfortunate model that many of us have seen in our fathers and may be trying, half-heartedly or wholeheartedly, to imitate is *the Autocrat*. Dad is the Boss around here, and don't you forget it. The Resident Caliph, King-of-the-Mountain . . . in stressful moments sometimes even known as Dictator, Tyrant, and other pejorative titles.

Actually, that's pushing it a bit too far, because most Autocrats do love their loyal subjects. They are not wanting to play Attila the Hun; they simply want to do a thorough job of taking care of their wives and children, and that means calling the shots. Almost all the shots. After all, it's their name on the mailbox, and they are not going to let their family suffer for lack of leadership.

This requires a good deal of effort on their part. Setting the budget . . . choosing the apartment or home . . . allowing or denying various activities, especially as they relate to discretionary income . . . setting standards on any number of things from school grades to church attendance to length of hair and hemlines to choice of music.

Add all this to the rigors of an eight-hour day at the office or plant, and you can see why some dads just aren't up to it.

But others are. They have a keen sense of answerability to the community, to God, and to themselves for the state of their household. Also, there is often family pride at stake. *We Johnsons do things a certain way* — the right way, and that's that.

Most families run very smoothly with a strong patriarch. That's one of the advantages of the system. I have a friend now nearing forty who, at a recent all-day family reunion, was directly ordered by his father not to begin washing his car because the noon meal would be ready within half an hour. My friend followed his deeply ingrained habit and promptly obeyed. The father wasn't trying to put down his son, now fully grown with a wife and three children of his own. He was just taking charge as he always had, ensuring that this family would continue to function smoothly!

Maybe your father was an Autocrat. Maybe he was an Abdicator. Maybe he was a variation of one or the other.

Maybe your father was the greatest. Maybe he tried hard but was preoccupied with other things and left a lot of gaps as a result. Maybe, to be honest, he was a downright flop.

Or maybe you grew up without a dad, and thus the preceding section has little relevance to you. In that case, your image of the male adult in the home is especially blurry.

Whatever — it's not likely that any one man can exemplify everything we need to know about husbanding. Our fathers made mistakes. And even when they handled things right, we weren't paying attention or couldn't appreciate the wisdom of their moves much of the time. We need help. We need a clearer understanding of our job in order not to perpetuate the sins of the fathers upon the third and fourth generations.

The Invisible Province

Remember your wedding gifts? That mountain of exquisite paper and ribbon filled with all manner of towels, dishes, and wall hangings that sent your bride into ecstasy?

You stood at her side, smiling and oohing appropriately as she opened each one. People had been most generous to the two of you. Yet . . . their generosity seemed rather slanted, didn't it? The gifts tended toward the housewifely side. Nobody had the common sense to give you a hacksaw, or a quarter-inch drill for putting up those curtain rods in a couple of weeks. Just toasters and queen-size sheets.

The greatest gift of that day, however, was not wrapped in metallic paper and two-tone ribbon. It was an intangible, as masculine as it is feminine, and intended to outlast both toasters and hacksaws. Without meaning to be melodramatic, let me state it clearly: *God has given you and your wife a unique, irreplaceable gift — your home*. The sum total of your togetherness. The atmosphere created by the two of you. The union, the entity created by the merger of your life and hers.

That entity may be housed in a one-bedroom apartment, a suburban split-level, or a fifty-year-old farmhouse with high ceilings and drafty windows. It may or may not have been extended by now to include one, two, or more children. It may have a solid financial base, or it may be severely pinched to make ends meet. The externals that surround the gift of your home are important, but not as important as the gift itself, the special thing God brought into being — your common life and relationship.

It's your base of operations. It's your foundation. It's your shelter from all the nasty people in the world. It's your arena for creativity, for expression, for mutual fulfillment. It is a divine work of art — "what God hath joined together."

It's not yours alone. Neither is it exclusively hers. It belongs to both of you. The apostle Peter calls you "joint heirs of the grace of life" (1 Peter 3:7 RSV). He's talking about procreation, yes. He's saying that it takes both of you to create new life. You are joint heirs of that particular miracle. But in a broader sense, I believe he's saying that married life . . . the home . . . the household . . . is something that belongs to both of you, that both of you create and enjoy, and that neither of you can usurp as your own private possession.

This gift is both glorious and fragile, enduring yet not automatic. And here is where we make our mistake. We start taking our home, our province, for granted. We assume it will always be there. Because it is so fundamental, we think it will hold up on its own. We can always go home, and home will always be home.

Not so. The unattended household has a way of degenerating and coming back to haunt us. We go steaming along our way, climbing our corporation ladders, pushing and getting pushed around in the modern bedlam — then we come home to collapse and recuperate. . . .

And it's not home. Something's wrong. Things are just as ragged here as they were out there. The relationship with our wife has deteriorated, and we hadn't even noticed. And now we desperately need the solace of that relationship, and it's gone, or at least rather seriously dissipated.

Meanwhile, she's hurting as badly as we are. Whether she spends her daytime hours in the house or away at an office, store, hospital, or school, she still needs many of the same things we need — togetherness, understanding, communication, lack of pressure, a place and a mate to facilitate recycling.

That's why husbanding requires *time* and *attention*. A lot of married men weren't thinking about that the night they proposed. They were thinking only about romance and sex and peer expectations and how to get out of doing laundry. Michael Novak, writing in *Harper's* magazine, says rather caustically:

> The central idea of our foggy way of life . . . is that life is solitary and brief, and that its aim is self-fulfillment. Next come beliefs in establishing the imperium of the self. . . . Autonomy we understand to mean protection of our inner kingdom — protection around the self from intrusions of chance, irrationality, necessity, and other persons. ("My self, my castle.") In such a vision of the self, marriage is merely an alliance. It entails as minimal an abridgment of inner privacy as one partner or the other may allow. Children are not a welcome responsibility, for to have children is, plainly, to cease being a child oneself.[1]

In contrast, the household God intends is a kingdom of two or more persons, and no medieval prince was ever so richly endowed. It is a fortress for the protection of love and Christian growth. The drawbridges are down to all who share the values of the kingdom, but they are fast shut against those who would destroy it.

Novak continues his analysis of modern marriage:

> People say of marriage that it is boring, when what they mean is that it terrifies them: too many and too deep are its searing revelations, its angers, its rages, its hates, and its loves. They say of marriage that it is deadening, when what they mean is that it drives us beyond adolescent fantasies and romantic dreams. They say of children that they are

piranhas, eels, brats, snots, when what they mean
is that the importance of parents with respect to the
future of their children is now known with greater
clarity and exactitude than ever before.[2]

The more we value our home, the province God has
given us, the more concerned we are that it thrive. It
becomes apparent that the realm must come under some
sort of organization, some kind of management to enable
the people on the inside to reach their full potential while
the enemies on the outside are held at bay.

God thought of that. He thought of it right at the
beginning when he bequeathed to Adam and Eve the first
home. He asked them both to "be fruitful and multiply,
and fill the earth and subdue it" (Gen. 1:28). This magnificent task began with Adam being asked to name each
animal (2:19). As for Eve, God called her Adam's
"helper" (2:18).

Two roles thus begin to emerge at this early time, even
before the Temptation and Fall recorded in Genesis 3.
The roles are reinforced in the New Testament, where
husbands are explicitly called "the head" (Eph. 5:23).

If you're a woman reading this (why are you reading
this book?!), or if you're a man who's at all conscious of
the current push for female equality, you're probably
starting to tense up right now. Is God a male chauvinist?
Why the man? And what's a "head"? How do "heads"
relate to "helpers"? Is one better than the other?

I think I can answer those questions without being
chauvinistic and without twisting Scripture. But it will
take all of chapter 2 (and maybe more!) to do so. I'll say
this much right here: Headship is not what you're probably thinking. It's a fairly radical idea.

[1]Michael Novak, "The Family Out of Favor," *Harper's*, 252, no. 1511
(April 1976), p. 39.
[2]Ibid., p. 42.

2

Leading
by Enabling

2

Leading
by Enabling

I was in San Francisco on a business trip during their somewhat notorious 1976 strike by municipal workers. Bus drivers, museum guards, trash collectors, and maintenance people at various city buildings had been off their jobs for about three weeks, and things were getting a little ugly.

There had been some pushing and shoving at several City Hall demonstrations as the public servants insisted on more money while the city council insisted it was broke. The situation had deteriorated to the level of bomb scares at the airport — which is what accounted for the rather strange announcement I heard as I walked up the concourse toward the baggage claim: "The restrooms have now been cleared and are again available for use," or some such words.

I didn't know enough about the local issues at stake to side with either the union or the city. But while waiting for my suitcase, I began musing about the rather curious term *public servant*. Obviously a misnomer. Servants don't haggle over wages, demand certain working hours and holidays, or walk off and quit in order to get their way. At least not the servants I've read about, especially in New Testament times.

I suppose that was part of the point of the strike: The "public servants" were tired of being treated like servants (according to their view of the facts) and wanted to be treated like something considerably higher.

Jesus once faced a situation in which a couple of his disciples initiated what might be called a bargaining session on their future working conditions. Actually, their designated negotiator was their mother (how can a boss get rough with anybody's mother, huh?), and the rhetoric was cordial as Mrs. Zebedee presented her case.

But Jesus took the occasion to make some startling statements about roles and relationships in the kingdom of God. He said:

> You know that the rulers of the Gentiles lord it over them, and their high officials exercise authority over them. Not so with you. Instead, whoever wants to become great among you must be your servant, and whoever wants to be first must be your slave — just as the Son of Man did not come to be served, but to serve, and to give his life a ransom for many (Matt. 20:25–28).

I don't think George Meany would like that. Neither, for that matter, would the American Management Association. Jesus is making a scramble of a whole set of preconceptions here, and he admits that the Gentiles aren't on his wavelength at all. That's right; we're not.

But what he is saying is that in *his* set of values, the Big Man is the slave. If you want to get to the top, stop trying to climb and start serving. The quest for power, he says, is all backwards; the only route to fulfillment is to abandon your rights.

The truth is that in our civilized society we've all but forgotten what a servant is and does. That's why we can call unionized municipal workers public servants and not realize the absurdity. A real servant is a human being who has lost everything — his freedom, his power, his prestige, and in ancient cultures, sometimes even his name. He was known commonly as "the slave of _____," symbolizing his total ownership by his master. Whatever the master ordered, he did, no matter how difficult, at what hour of the day or night, or with what hazards. He served, period.

Jesus told the ambitious James and John that the road to greatness in God's scheme of things was a road of serving. He didn't even let himself off the hook. "The Son of man . . . came to serve," he said.

The Bible doesn't say how the two brothers (and mama) reacted to that rather deflating news. But I know how we in the modern church have reacted. We have done our best to avoid the call to servanthood.

One thing we've done is to switch words. The King James Version generally does not say "serving." It says "ministry" instead. "Whosoever will be great among you, let him be your minister" (Matt. 20:26). Ah, that has a little more class to it. Any Christian parent is proud when his or her offspring announces, "I think I'm going to study for the ministry." How nice. He's on his way toward respectability.

Another King James word for *servant* is *deacon*. Again, we've institutionalized something that in the beginning was meant to be plain, honest, hard work for the benefit of the rest of the body of Christ. The first deacons were chosen in Acts 6 to be cooks and waiters for a group of elderly women. (Talk about Women's Liberation!) Read it for yourself. The name *deacon* comes to us straight from the Greek *diakoneō* — to serve.

About this time you're starting to think, *This makes no sense at all. If the leaders of the church — and even Jesus himself — are nothing more than servants, who's in charge of things?! Somebody's got to be the leader.*

You're right. Someone has to lead. And that someone is the servant.

Perhaps the most extraordinary thing Jesus ever did was what he did after they'd finished eating the Last Supper. Everyone was sitting around enjoying a second cup of coffee (or whatever came last in the meal) when all of a sudden the Son of God "got up . . . took off his outer clothing, and wrapped a towel around his waist" (John 13:4).

What's going on?

"After that, he poured water into a basin and began to wash his disciples' feet, drying them with the towel that was wrapped around him" (13:5).

Crazy!

Washing guests' feet was a scum job if there ever was one, a drudgery even slaves did not greet with enthusiasm. Peter's brain was reeling with the incongruity of it all, and he said so. But Jesus was not going to stop.

Finally, the washing was finished. "He put on his clothes and returned to his place. 'Do you understand what I have done for you?' he asked them" (13:12).

A simple question.

NO. They didn't have the slightest notion. (Neither do we. We've read this story dozens of times, and most of us still don't get it.)

So he explained.

> You call me "Teacher" and "Lord," and rightly so,
> for that is what I am. Now that I, your Lord and

Teacher, have washed your feet, you also should wash one another's feet. I have set you an example that you should do as I have done for you. I tell you the truth, no servant is greater than his master, nor is a messenger greater than the one who sent him. Once you know these things, you will be blessed if you do them (13:13–17).

Jesus thus created a new, seemingly schizophrenic role: the leader/servant. The chief/Indian. The honcho/peon. He acknowledged the need for leadership. Jesus was not an anarchist. But neither was he willing to tolerate the all-too-frequent abuses of power. Leadership, he said, is earned, is indeed made possible only by serving.

We have a long way to go to implement this in the church. We have a long way to go to implement it in many of our homes as well.

We are rather adept at pretending to serve while doing the opposite. As I write this, the current television commercials have fresh-faced teen-age employees of a certain fast-food empire smiling into the camera and singing, "We do it all for you!" I happen to live about fifteen miles from that empire's international headquarters, and I must say it's a rather impressive piece of architecture on a rather valuable piece of real estate right beside the tollway. They're obviously not doing it *all* for me. The language is the language of servanthood, but the facts are something else.

We Christians play the same games. Juan Carlos Ortiz, the insightful Buenos Aires pastor, tells in his book *Disciple:*

Once I was in a meeting where someone was introduced with great fanfare. The organ played and the spotlights came on as someone announced, "And now, the great servant of God, _____."

If he was great, he was not a servant. And if he was a servant, he was not great. Servants are people who understand that they are worthy of nothing.
. . .

May God help us to do with joy what servants in His Kingdom do.[1]

What is a husband?

It is with this understanding that we must now begin to define what Paul meant when he called the husband "the head." We must not allow secularist management consultants or family psychologists to write our definitions. We must not succumb to the prevailing haphazard opinions of our society.

We must not be swayed even by what we perceive to be "efficient." Efficiency is a great god in most of our lives, and students of human relationships have done much research to find the best ways for the average stubborn bunch of people to get along with each other, to get something accomplished instead of spending nine-to-five at one another's throats. Without modern efficiency methods, this country wouldn't be half as productive as it is.

But certain things are different in the kingdom ruled by love. When the Lord of the kingdom has succeeded in purging us of our basic hostilities toward one another, we are then freed to become one another's servants and not get up-tight about it. Our egos do not have to be pampered. We have chosen a radical, paradoxical road to greatness.

And the place where all this must begin is at home. The head of a Christian household is the man who has given himself to serve his wife and his children, if any. Why? Because he loves them. He is the guy who enables things to succeed. He is the guy who plans ahead so schedules mesh. He is the guy who figures out what's causing tension and then moves to relieve it. He is solution-oriented.

And if the solution involves getting his hands dirty, so be it. He's not on a pedestal. He's not hung up about washing feet . . . or windows, or little boys' elbows. He is not worried about being respected. He is not concerned about prestige. He is concerned only about serving his God-given province.

Do you know any husbands like that?

The greatest challenge (so far) to my leader/servant-hood began on March 3, 1975, at about nine o'clock at night. Our 2½-year-old son was soundly asleep in his crib, and I was enjoying *Time* magazine in the living room. Outside, the Illinois winter was finishing its last gusts. It was one of those nice, quiet evenings that would be even nicer if they'd stay that way.

I was getting back toward the business section when the front door opened and my very pregnant wife came in from her biweekly visit to the obstetrician. She said not a word — she didn't even take off her coat — but walked straight to a chair across from me and slumped. There was shock on her face, but it was her special kind of mock-shock that she puts on whenever she wants to make sure I'm paying attention before she speaks.

I went along with the drama. I waited. Finally, I grinned and said, "Okay — what happened?"

"Heitzler thinks he hears two heartbeats."

"You're kidding."

"No."

A set of X-rays at the hospital tomorrow morning would tell for sure, but suddenly we already knew we were having twins. This weird pregnancy now made sense — the nausea that wouldn't go away, all the urgent rushes to the bathroom during supper (Grace's morning sickness always struck around 5:00 P.M.), the rather sudden inflation of her middle starting at about the fifth month, and more recently the mysterious swelling of her feet and ankles, which had seemed for all the world like diabetes until the tests turned out negative.

We sat there talking, staring, and crying. She gave me a second-by-second replay of how the nurse had first discovered the two heartbeats and then how excited Dr. Heitzler had gotten, pushing with his stethoscope here and there in search of thump-thumps until she thought her abdomen was going to split open on the spot.

After another dozen exclamations ("Wow!" "This is unbelievable." "Wow!"), we started tracing the family trees in search of other cases of multiple births. None. We were unique.

Finally we snapped back to reality. We had approximately six weeks to get ready for two new people in our lives. Nathan would have to be shifted immediately to a regular bed so his crib could be added to the one we'd already bought at a garage sale. Grace would have to drop her Sunday school teaching immediately instead of later, since the doctor had ordered complete bed rest from here on. Our minds were swimming at all the adjustments to be made in six short weeks, provided the twins didn't arrive early, as twins often do.

On March 14 — eleven days later — Rhonda Joy and Tricia Dawn made their entrance.

My memories of that first year are pretty much a blur. Any parent of twins will tell you that if you can survive the first year, you're probably going to make it the rest of the way. We got to the place where Grace would handle the first nighttime feeding — whichever baby awakened first — and I would take the second. The weary breakfast conversation the next morning would invariably go, "Well, 'my' baby lasted till 3:45 — how long did 'yours' go?" Throughout the day, of course, simultaneous feedings were necessary to preserve sanity.

The rewards for all this came whenever we mustered the energy to take the family out in public. People would swarm around, ooh and ahh, and ask dumb questions like "Are they twins?" At such times Grace and I would forget about all the work and stand back to appreciate the beauty of God's double gift.

However, the simple process of getting the family ready to go anywhere made these times precarious at best. Long after most procedures of the week had been tamed, Sunday morning remained my nemesis. Getting five people fed, dressed, and in the car on time without two or three episodes of tears (children) or frustrated anger (adults) seemed virtually impossible.

I remember in particular one Sunday not long before the twins' first birthday. It wasn't one of the worst, but it was not the best either. My difficulty was internal; I was feeling that the entire weekend so far had been nothing but children, children, children, and I had been trying to give each of them time and give Grace some relief — but underneath, I really wanted to get at some house jobs and reorganize my makeshift office in the basement and do what *I* wanted to do. I wanted to make efficient use of my time.

Children, you may have noticed, are not particularly geared to that abstraction known as efficiency.

By Sunday morning my inner tendons were getting tighter and tighter. I gritted my way through the breakfast hour and the dressing process, helping Nathan get ready while Grace dressed the girls. A last-minute messy diaper was changed without too much trauma. We even managed to get all three into snowsuits and out to the car with only minor skirmishes.

But I was in no shape for church. I felt like I had done

my duty in spite of myself. We dropped the girls at the nursery, took Nathan to his toddler group, and Grace went on to one of the adult elective classes. I seriously considered finding something else to do until the worship hour. I mainly wanted just to sit and do a little silent fuming. I was not particularly interested in the pronouncements of any Sunday school teacher.

I indulged in my private little muddle for a few minutes, but it didn't feel as good as I had hoped. I finally made a late entrance into the class and found a seat beside Grace.

The text for the morning was Philippians 2. I listened as the Scripture was read:

> Do nothing out of selfish ambition or vain conceit, but in humility consider others better than yourselves. Each of you should not look only to your own interests, but also to the interests of others. Your attitude should be the same as that of Christ Jesus: Who, being in very nature God, did not consider equality with God something to be grasped, but made himself nothing, *taking the very nature of a servant,* being made in human likeness. And being found in appearance as a man, he humbled himself and became obedient to death — even death on a cross! (2:3–8).

The teacher didn't need to say a word. The apostle had already shot me down. *Servanthood, Dean! All weekend you've been refusing to be a servant, and that's why you're so tight. You've forgotten that God has made you the servant of Nathan and Rhonda and Tricia, and Grace as well. No wonder the household is about to explode.*

A friend of mine, Dick Foth, who leads/serves a church near the University of Illinois campus in Urbana, says, "What are the true signs of spiritual maturity? If a poll were taken of Christians, how would they answer? I have a feeling they would cite such things as the ability to pray, to expound Scripture, to witness, to manifest dramatic gifts of the Holy Spirit — healings, miracles, that sort of thing."

Dick doesn't object to those, and neither do I. But in his opinion, "The acid test of spiritual maturity is *relationships*. If my Christianity does not profoundly affect my relationship with my wife, with my children, with the board of my church, with the members of my congregation — then I'm not as mature as I might like to think."

The Jesus Movement of the early seventies generated a lot of slogans — some corny, others pretty good. The one I liked best was SERVE THE LORD, SERVE THE PEOPLE.

The second half is but a practical translation of the first. Both amount to the same thing. In my role as a Christian husband, as head of the unique gift I call home, SERVE THE LORD, SERVE THE HOUSEHOLD is not a bad definition of my job.

[1]Juan Carlos Ortiz, *Disciple* (Carol Stream, Ill.: Creation House, 1975), p. 39.

3

People
Who Need
People

3

People
Who Need
People

You've heard the following sentence so often you've gotten numb to it. It's become a cliche. But God said it, and it's profound. Perhaps some meaning can be injected into it.

Here it is:

"It is not good that the man should be alone" (Gen. 2:18).

Run it through your brain a couple more times. *It is not good that the man should be alone.*

I believe this is something more than just an excuse for getting married. I believe God is making a fundamental observation about the nature of human beings. He is saying something like this: "I could have made people any number of different ways, but I happen to have chosen to make people so that they need other people. A human being by himself — whether he admits it or not — is going to have a tougher time of it."

It becomes fairly clear after a few moments of thought

that God is talking about something more than physical proximity. Simply being in the presence of other people is not the answer. We have all had the experience of being intensely lonely at a crowded party. In fact, some sociologists have observed that the more compacted we become geographically, the more distant we are interpersonally. Most farmers know and relate to the family a mile down the gravel road better than most high-rise apartment dwellers do to the couple behind the next door.

So Genesis 2:18 cannot mean that the simple act of living with your wife under the same roof takes care of the disadvantages of aloneness.

Neither, for that matter, can it mean that the single person who lives by himself is automatically shut out from the blessings of relationship.

What God is saying is that people — men, women, marrieds, singles, everybody — are in need of interaction with other people, and to deny ourselves that interaction is "not good."

There are a lot of single adults who understand this very deeply and have gone out of their way to establish solid, meaningful lines of communication with others.

And there are a lot of husbands (and wives) who, physical proximity notwithstanding, are living alone.

Why is aloneness "not good"?

The need for togetherness implanted by God into the human race there in Eden runs all through our existence from bottom to top. We obviously need each other for physical reasons, to help each other acquire food, clothing, and shelter. The man who gets married essentially to have a cook and seamstress is operating on this low level.

Our greater needs lie in the intangibles. We can cook our own meals and iron our own shirts far easier than we can effectively criticize our own ideas or plan our own futures. Another way of saying this is that we all need *feedback*, someone to bounce things back to us, someone to encourage us when we need it — and deflate us when we need it. Someone to say things like:

"That's a fantastic idea. You're brilliant."

Or: "Yes, but what about————?"

Or: "I was reading something about that the other day; did you know ————?"

Or: "You've got to be kidding!"

At the same time, we husbands can make a contribution by listening to and interacting with our wives' thoughts, ideas, brainstorms, and dreams. It's true not only on the job but also at home: Two heads really are better than one.

All of this is not to deny the value of solitude. The Scriptures are all in favor of times for reflection, for getting away from other people to regain one's perspective. Moses, for example, spent several forty-day spells alone with his God.

But was that really aloneness? Perhaps it was the greatest form of encounter possible. Moses was not really alone. He was face-to-face with another Being, and all his powers of concentration were undoubtedly focused on the dialogue.

We put aloneness furthest from us when we are locked in serious encounter with just one other person, divine or human. This is the wonder of prayer. It is also the wonder of Christian marriage. The more persons we try to relate to simultaneously, the more the bonds begin to break up and the more we slip off toward aloneness again, e.g., the crowded party.

"What'd you do today?"

What if we were to take a poll of our wives and ask them to complete this sentence:

The greatest evidence that my husband loves me is that:

- ☐ he spends money on me.
- ☐ he gives great sex.
- ☐ he talks.

I think we know what the answer would be. Number three would win by a landslide.

Wives seek conversation. They're frustrated when they don't get it. They can endure tight budgets and headaches at bedtime far easier than suppertime silence.

Why?

If you're thinking, *Because all women are gabby,* shame on you. There are some legitimate reasons.

1. A wife is a human being, just like you. And as we've already noted, God didn't program human beings for aloneness. He programed us, male and female, for togetherness, companionship, interaction.

2. A wife is understandably curious about the goings-on of her leader/servant. Assuming she subscribes to the scriptural roles described in the previous chapter, she views you as fairly strategic to the Invisible Province with which the two of you have been gifted. She's looking to you for direction — not in the form of commands or policy statements, but in the subtleties of open conversation and, even more importantly, the actions of servanthood.

Perhaps the whole modern controversy among many Christians about the submission of wives to husbands would not be so heated if we paid more attention to the *oneness* God intends in marriage. It seems to me that the submission passage of Ephesians 5 is perhaps God's emergency provision, a backup measure for those times when a decision's got to be made and we haven't come to consensus with our wives. In cases of deadlock, yes, the husband has to call the shot. But was the deadlock really necessary?

Managers in business give high priority to generating a team atmosphere among workers, a sense of common task, so that problems are approached from a basis of "We ought to . . ." instead of "The boss says. . . ." If in our marriages the goals of *union, oneness, concurrence,* and *consensus* were more central, perhaps we wouldn't need to talk so much about submission. If we truly believed that God intends for two people to become one, there wouldn't be so many confrontations to negotiate. Because if we and our wives are of one mind on a question, no one has to submit. We move ahead in agreement.

And the merger of two sets of opinions takes place largely through conversation.

3. If your wife is the kind who's home all day, she doesn't encounter many adults. She's probably a mother; she lives in the world of children for a major portion of each week. Most of the adults she's with for any length of time are *very* similar to her — namely, other mothers at home with children.

So here you come at five o'clock. You're sort of a novelty. You're male instead of female. And you've been in an adult world all day. You've been in the world of ideas, machines, money, and all sorts of interesting things. You make for a nice change of pace in her day. You're her window to a lot of places, people, and events that otherwise are inaccessible to her.

"But I'm *tired* when I get home from work," you say. "I've been fighting the expressway traffic for forty-five minutes, and the pressures of my job are still swirling through my head, and I'm just not in the mood to walk in and be an instantly charming conversationalist."

That's probably true. A lot of us work in jobs that won't turn off with a switch. It takes us a while to come down, to remember that there's always tomorrow and that the work will still be there.

Thus the evening meal may not be the best communication time for you and your wife. There's no rule that says it has to be. There are lots of other options. I know one couple who get up at 4:30 A.M. every day so they can exercise and then enjoy a long, leisurely breakfast together before heading for work!

What is important is that you and your wife not live your lives in aloneness. The details are up to you.

Actually, your communication goes far deeper than "What'd you do today?" The everyday places you've been, people you've seen, and catastrophes you've avoided are starting points, of course. But they're not enough. In fact, they can get rather boring unless you both can place all this minutiae against the backdrop of a deeper sharing of plans, feelings, wishes, hopes, fears, aspirations, and dreams. A lot of husbands yawn through their wives' descriptions of the morning coffee klatsch, not because the klatsch itself was a bore but because the husband has no feeling for why this might be important to his wife. He hardly knows the other families in the neighborhood; maybe he can't even connect faces with the names his wife is mentioning. They're nonpersons to him. So no wonder he's out of sync with the klatsch discussion of vacation spots or fancy restaurants, because he's not really aware of his wife's secret wishes, likes, and dislikes on those topics.

The New Testament even hints in 1 Corinthians 14:35 that husbands and wives should get into Christian belief and doctrine together. Paul (for whatever reason) asked the first-century women to keep silent in the church meetings — but not to bury their questions. "They should ask their own husbands at home," he wrote.

When was the last time you and your wife had a theological discussion?

Finding the time

The most unfortunate thing about husband-wife communication is that its absence doesn't cause immediate repercussions. Your stomach doesn't growl as it does when you miss a meal. You don't go stumbling through the next day as you do after getting to bed at three or three-thirty in the morning. Therefore, it's fairly easy to stay busy with more mundane things and never get around to genuine meeting of minds.

But if you're convinced that you *need* her and she *needs* you, that it is not good to live alone, then you'll find the time. In addition to the two options already mentioned — evening mealtime and early morning — here are some others:

• *Late at night,* as you're going to sleep (unless you're the type who's "out" the minute you hit the bed). Naturally, some nights you're going to be engaged in nonverbal communication (more about that in chapter 9), but what about the other nights?

• *Driving time* — a beautiful set-up for talking about all kinds of things. You're sitting there together, you can't do much else — why not get in some quality time with each other? Long trips are great, but even the short runs to shopping centers, to church, to friends' houses are good opportunities to talk.

• *Restaurants.* The big, splashy ones, yes, but also the corner coffee shops where you can get two pecan rolls and two cups of coffee for two bucks or less . . . and sit for an hour if you like.

• *Vacations.* The point of a vacation is not only to *do* some neat things and *avoid* the old grind, but also to *be with* each other for greater chunks of time than is possible in the normal week. Vacations are great for getting into those heavy topics that otherwise take too long.

• *"Appointments."* If the above situations aren't enough, there's nothing wrong with blocking out a certain hour each week simply to sit down together in the living room, turn off the TV, and talk. You think that sounds artificial and awkward? Not if you believe that communicating with your wife is at least as important as seeing your doctor. One is as easy to postpone as the other, but in both cases, you'll eventually wish you hadn't.

Finding the time becomes at least 100 percent more difficult as soon as children arrive on the scene. Grace and I'd been married four years when we concluded that the Lord wanted us to help resolve a particular situation in my family by inviting my thirteen-year-old niece to come live with us. We'd been used to totally free and open times of conversation during two meals each day, plus hours and hours of additional time on the weekends.

All of a sudden there were three plates at the table, not two. All of a sudden there was a thirteen-year-old mind listening to everything we said. We immediately shifted, of course, from Dean/Grace conversation to Dean/Vickie and Grace/Vickie conversation: school, swimming, the youth group at church, guys, clothes . . . all important parts of her world. We knew we needed to build a lot of bridges toward her, and mealtimes were natural for working at this.

But when were Grace and I to talk about family finances?

When were we to talk about the pressures of my job (which were considerable that particular year)?

When were we to talk about how we both felt about Vickie? Whether we'd made the right decision on her most recent request? Whether she was feeling wanted and loved? What we ought to be doing differently?

Obviously, not at the supper table.

We simply had to carve out times to be alone and communicate, let our hair down, get used to being the instant parents of a teen-ager, coordinate our decision-making, and reassure each other of our love and gratitude for what the other person was contributing to this venture.

When a newborn baby comes into your home, of course, it's not such a shock to your communication patterns at the beginning. You're super-busy, of course, but you can talk *while* you're taking care of an infant.

In less than a year, though, your son or daughter is in a high chair at the table. He still doesn't understand what you're saying, but it's getting a bit more difficult to bare your soul to your wife while you're also trying to con Li'l Punkin' into downing his strained spinach. Somehow there's a distraction factor in there somewhere.

Between ages two and three, your youngster begins picking up the simple parts of table conversation. At our house there are rather hilarious efforts to talk past our kids either by spelling out the key words ("Keep the c-o-o-k-i-e-s out of sight until she's finished her mashed potatoes.") or by using Parent Double-talk ("The eldest will need to participate in a cleansing soon after the conclusion of this repast." Translation: "Nathan's taking a bath after supper.").

Eventually, of course, your kids learn how to spell and also how to translate, and mom and dad have to find other times and places for saying what needs to be said to each other. The danger here is that, due to children or any number of other reasons (work schedules, for example), you and your wife don't manage to find enough time for strictly adult-level communication. That is a tragedy.

Blessed are the peacemakers

Even with adequate time and the best of intentions, there will be times when the communication lines get snarled. The two of you simply aren't going to be in harmony every moment of your married lives. We have all experienced disagreement and conflict; we know how rotten it feels. I can stand a difference of opinion or even a simple misunderstanding with anyone in the world easier than with Grace. When the two of us have gotten crosswise on an issue, regardless of what it is, I'm miserable.

An important question I ask myself whenever faced with a marital misunderstanding is, "Is this whole problem real or imagined? Did she really intend to cause me this grief? Or was it an accident?"

The majority of times, it was an accident. Either —

• We hadn't taken time to talk things through thoroughly; we were in a hurry, so we cut the conversation short, or maybe we didn't talk at all. We just *assumed* we knew what was in the other person's head.

• Or we fell into blurring the distinction between idea and person. We started wrapping up our ego with the position we were defending. It was no longer a question of whether the bedroom would look better in blue or beige; it was a question of whose will was stronger. In such a moment, we both have forgotten about our calling to be servants of each other.

Sven Wahlroos, in his book *Family Communication*, lists a number of what he calls "unfair techniques" that husbands and wives often employ. How many of the following sound vaguely familiar?

• *"Am I supposed to jump up and down and lick your boots?"* Unfair Technique I: Pretending that the other person has made an unreasonable statement or demand.

• *"You did it only because you feel guilty."* Unfair Technique II: Mind reading, psychologizing, jumping to conclusions; pretending that one single motive constitutes complete motivation; divination.

46

- *"Anyway, look how filthy this room is!"* Unfair Technique III: Switching the subject; using counter-accusations.
- *"And furthermore. . . ."* Unfair Technique IV: Bringing up more than one accusation at a time; the kitchen sink attack.
- *"I try much harder than you."* Unfair Technique V: Bragging, or playing the numbers game.
- *"Why make a big deal out of nothing?"* Unfair Technique VI: Using logic to hide from emotional reality.
- *"But that's not true. I didn't. . . ."* Unfair Technique VII: Interrupting.
- *"All right, we'll see what you say when I divorce you!"* Unfair Technique VIII: Using the atom bomb, the bull in the china shop; intimidating, yelling, screaming, and "exploding."
- *"You're just like your father, that no-good bum."* Unfair Technique IX: Blaming the partner for something he cannot help or cannot do anything about now, or for something you do yourself; refusing to forgive.
- *"How can you be so stupid?"* Unfair Technique X: Humiliating the partner; using insults and epithets, rubbing in; exposing dirty linen in public, comparing unfavorably.
- *"That's all in your mind."* Unfair Technique XI: Crazy-making; "bugging"; unpredictability.
- *"Boo-hoo, boo-hoo."* Unfair Technique XII: Having one's feelings hurt at the drop of a hat; guilt induction; the destructive use of crying.
- *"Sure, sure, I'll bet."* Unfair Technique XIII: The use of sarcasm and ridicule.
- *"————"* Unfair Technique XIV: Silence, ignoring, sulking, pouting; "cold-shoulder treatment."[1]

The amazing thing to me is that we unleash such comments on the one person whom we love most in all the world — when our sense of common courtesy would prevent us from doing the same to a secretary, a store clerk, or a fellow worker. Any foreman or manager worth his salt knows that there's a right and a wrong way to deal with someone who disagrees with him. Why is it that we can come home and let our mouths say things we'd never dare say to casual acquaintances?

What is *really* interesting is to watch what happens when we put the two together — when we're with our wives and other people in a social situation. A tremendous amount of classified information can be learned just by listening to how husbands and wives talk to and about each other in public. I have, in the course of a single evening, heard apparently happily married spouses cut each other down four, five, and six times. Things like:

"Wow, I didn't think George was ever going to find this place tonight — he went around and around the block; he even forgot the paper where I'd written the directions."

"Oh, look at these hors d'oeuvres. Hey, Joyce, wanna see some good food for a change?'

"How d'ya like my wife's $40 hairdo?"

The American brand of humor, in fact, is built largely upon sarcasm and making the other person look foolish. (In contrast, humor in other parts of the world is more often based on things like word plays and the preposterous, with the result that American jokes often seem crude and mean by comparison.)

The Christian husband is the guy who resists the temptation to use a wife joke to get a laugh. If he has a bone to pick with his wife, he does it straightforwardly and in private. As Paul wrote in Ephesians 5:29,33, "After all, no one ever hated" (shall we add "or embarrassed"?) "his own body, but he feeds and cares for it, just as Christ does the church — for we are members of his body. . . . Each one of you also must love his wife as he loves himself."

I imagine Christ could crack quite a lot of very funny jokes about the imperfections of the church. But he doesn't. He loves us too much.

The evidence of love is often contained in words. Public words, private words. Words *to* our wives, words *about* our wives. Words — the right kind of honest and affirming words — are the stepping stones that lead us from the tragedy of aloneness. They are the stones with which we build the castle of marriage.

[1]Sven Wahlroos, *Family Communication* (New York: Macmillan, 1974).

4

The Dance
of the
Dollars

4

The Dance
of the
Dollars

The first twenty-five years of our lives, according to an old sage whose name I've forgotten, our major shortage is *money*.

The next twenty-five years, our major shortage is *time*.

And the last twenty-five years, we're fighting hardest for *energy*.

There's a good chunk of truth in that — but I've got news for the wise man: the money problems don't evaporate on the twenty-fifth birthday. (And the time squeeze starts several years earlier, right?)

A shortage is a natural breeder of tension. We all know how easily our marriages can sputter, fume, and sizzle over the lack — real or imagined — of enough money to do what we and/or our wives want. Long after our sexual lives have been harmonized, our major career choices have been agreed upon, and the size of our family has been determined, we can still be hassling over money, with no solution in sight.

Our difficulty is usually a classic example of worrying about individual trees instead of the forest. How come groceries are so high? Why did she buy that new coat when she *knew* things were tight this month? A hefty six-month insurance premium is due, and there's no nest egg to take care of it.

And we react. We shoot from the hip. We launch into a harangue about holding down expenses. We bemoan the rising cost of living. We curse the Democrats, or the Republicans, as the case may be. To handle the current brushfire, we write a hot check and hope for the best. Or we run out to the friendly household finance corporation for a quick loan — at highway-robbery interest rates.

There has to be a better way.

Whose money?

The Bible, as you know, does not say that money is the root of all evil. (What it says in 1 Timothy 6:10 is that "the love of money is a root of all kinds of evil.") Money itself ought not to be a headache. It ought not to be a source of contention. Instead, it is one of our resources (along with time, energy, air, water, etc.), part of the raw material with which we build our lives. Money, I happen to believe, is another "good and perfect gift . . . from above, coming down from the Father of the heavenly lights" (James 1:17).

Don't think of God as too holy to touch the stuff. The Scriptures often speak of him as the Creator and Owner of the entire cosmos. His barrage of questions in Job 38–41 is essentially a litany of all that he controls.

And he has chosen to assign a few of his resources to you and your wife to administrate. He has given the two of you a combination of energy and intelligence, which you convert for forty hours or so each week into earnings.

You do a number of other things with your allotment of

energy and intelligence, of course, which don't translate into cash, e.g., mowing the lawn, fixing breakfast, playing racquetball, doing the laundry, etc. Each has its place.

Thus, we come to some premises:

1. Money is a good thing — it's one of God's gifts to us.

2. Since it's one of God's gifts, it needs to be used with care and thoughtfulness.

3. The gift of money is a *joint* gift, a joint asset. It belongs to the household, the unified life that you and your wife have set up.

And the practical question for the two of you boils down to:

What shall *we* do with *our* money?

I'm not just talking about whether you file a joint income tax return each year. And it's more than a matter of both of you signing the house mortgage papers. It is of strategic importance that at the very core of your two brains you *think* and *feel* in terms of common money. It belongs to both of you, and you're answerable to each other as well as to the Giver for how it's used or abused.

You don't have trouble thinking *our refrigerator*.

Or *our TV*.

Or *our children*.

Why not *our money?*

True, it implies that you and your wife have given up your independence. You're totally vulnerable to each other. She can run the household straight into bankruptcy. And so can you. But you love each other . . . you're committed to each other . . . you're watching out for each other's good . . . and that makes the crucial difference.

Lurking in the back of everyone's mind, of course, is *who actually earned the money*. Whose name was on the paycheck? Who actually invested his blood, sweat, and tears to generate that income? I have not only my energy but, unfortunately, a piece of my ego in those dollars. *I* did it. Other people may have been loafing the past two weeks, but *I* was getting things done, and here's the proof. I am a productive person. I'm carrying my own weight in this world.

So what's this bit about *our* money?!

If you are the sole wage earner of the household, you and your wife have simply made a decision that you will venture into the world of commerce and invest a major portion of yourself earning dollars while she invests a major portion of herself on other nonremunerative but equally important tasks. This arrangement, my friend, does *not* make you better than her. It says absolutely nothing about your value to the household or society at large in comparison with hers.

Your neighbors, friends, and business associates may *think* it does. Ours is such a money-hungry culture that the ability to earn money has become a popular gauge of one's worth. The more you earn, the more you're esteemed.

That is a particularly demeaning as well as non-Christian concept. If my value as a person rises or falls solely on my commercial value in this world, I'm in deep trouble. What happens if I get fired . . . or sick . . . or past sixty-five? I'm suddenly a nonperson.

We Christians have trouble resisting this pagan value-system. My wife continues to fret occasionally about the fact that she currently isn't generating any dollars. She was a teacher the first six years of our marriage, including a year when I was in graduate school and she was the sole dollar-producer. She may well return to the classroom in a few years when our children are in school, but for now, she's a full-time mother. We keep reminding each other that mothering is an extremely important and valuable part of our life together — more important that earning dollars, in fact. We'd give up my job and try to subsist off the land before we'd ever give up our kids. But Grace still keeps thinking about the days when she used to bring home a paycheck. So she has a ways to go to make her feelings match her Christian values.

I shouldn't talk — not until I've put myself to the test by turning the tables again as we did in graduate-school days, only on a permanent basis. Mike McGrady, a Long Island newspaper columnist, tells about such a life in his delightful book *The Kitchen Sink Papers*. After reaching a fairly high plateau in his profession, McGrady decided to shake things up and trade places with his wife, whose growing home furnishings business had the potential of supporting the family. Mike became the househusband, caring for their three children, while Corinne became the breadwinner. He describes how it felt to be handed his first weekly "allowance" of a hundred dollars for groceries and etcetera.

> It is an unpracticed exchange, accomplished awkwardly. I don't know which of us has more difficulty, which of us is more embarrassed. I guess Corinne handles her side of the exchange more smoothly than I do. . . .
>
> It is the easiest hundred dollars I've ever made. But the reversal feels strange. . . . This ritual, the giving of allowance by one human being to another, bespeaks whole planets of meaning; it has to do with independence, gratification, reward, punishment, resentment. The feelings are so intertwined that I doubt whether they can be fully understood until the situation is reversed. . . .
>
> My own reaction on receiving money — this first day and every week since then — has not been what I anticipated. It is not a pleasurable experience, not in the least. In fact, there is on my part

> inevitably an effort to minimize the transaction, to
> snatch up the check and stuff it into my wallet as
> rapidly as possible, to pretend that the transaction
> doesn't really matter. I can see, in Corinne, oppo-
> site tendencies, an effort to ceremonialize the offer-
> ing, to announce it in advance — "Ah, today is the
> day you get your allowance" — to make a produc-
> tion number out of locating the checkbook and the
> pen, to sign it with a flourish, to hand it over with a
> kiss.
>
> I know her feeling all too well.[1]

Throughout the book, the McGradys (who do not pretend to be Christians) can be seen edging toward an
our-money concept, although at the end they are still not
to the point of a joint checking account, except for certain
house expenses.

If both you and your wife work, you may be trapped all
the more in the rut of "My dollars are mine and hers are
hers." In such a mindset, money often equals clout. And
if a highly motivated, successful wife starts bringing
home the larger paycheck of the two (which is entirely
possible in these times), a threatened husband can go into
all manner of traumas.

The leader/servant of a Christian household is the
person who refuses to use his or her earning power as a
club, or even a small lever. He steadfastly resists the
culture's belief that money is power. He thanks God for
this gift, along with all others, and works with his spouse
to use it responsibly.

Now, back to the question: What shall *we* do with *our*
money?

A sizable pile of change

The biggest difficulty for most of us is not that we come
up with bad answers to that question. It's that we don't
take time to answer it at all. We don't plan; we just spend.

And when we don't have money to spend, we call it a cash flow problem and proceed to borrow so we can keep on spending.

A family exchequer is a larger, more complicated thing than we often realize. Many of us are running through the equivalent of a new Mercedes every year. We're spending money in twenty-five to thirty different categories, from housing to utilities to restaurants to gasoline.

The key to keeping control over that rather sizable pile of change . . . the key not only to staying out of financial trouble but *enjoying* God's gift to you as well . . . is for you and your wife to *agree in advance* how you're going to spend it. That process of saying "Here's what we have to work with, and here's what we're going to do with it" is called budgeting. If the word has a nasty odor to it, call it *planning your money* or whatever you like. Just do it.

You begin by finding out your monthly income. If you're on a regular payroll, it's easy. All it takes is a little arithmetic to convert your regular paycheck(s) to a monthly basis. If you're paid biweekly, for example, you simply multiply by twenty-six (the number of paychecks you get each year) and then divide by twelve.

(You had a small excuse for not budgeting before the invention of electronic calculators. But now, the old complaint about "doing all that figuring" is dead.)

Be sure to add any little extra sources of income you've got going on the side. Is your wife tutoring? Do you have a part-time or sometime job? Are there investment dividends to add on?

It gets a little messier if your income is not regular — if you're in business for yourself or if you're a salesman on commission. I know more than one such husband who uses this as an excuse not to budget. "I never know when the money's coming or how much. So I just have to fly by instinct."

Nonsense. If giant corporations can estimate their income on the basis of past records, you can too. You told the IRS what you made last year, didn't you? Take that figure and divide by twelve. Even if your money comes unevenly throughout the year, find the average monthly figure. (There are some tricks you can play in arranging the due-dates of certain bills to compensate for those variances in income. More about that later.)

Before you and your wife go any further — stop and thank the Lord for his gift. Think about all the people in the world making less than you are (there are probably billions of them). Tell the Lord how much you appreciate having this much money to work with, and that you're going to try to use it as responsibly as possible, and that you'd appreciate his guidance as you proceed.

Your first decision is how much you're going to return to the Lord directly. In Old Testament times, as you know, Jehovah set that figure for you: 10 percent. The New Testament doesn't lay down any hard quotas; instead, in keeping with its spiritual nature, it rather cheerfully urges us to "excel in this grace of giving" (2 Cor. 8:7). A little further on, Paul says, "Remember this: Whoever sows sparingly will also reap sparingly, and whoever sows generously will also reap generously. Each man should give what he has decided in his heart to give, not reluctantly or under compulsion . . ." (2 Cor. 9:6,7).

It was during my year of graduate school that Grace and I finally came to an understanding of this concept. We were on a rather stringent budget, and we had dutifully written a tithe into it — a 10 percent contribution to our church each payday. It was an automatic thing, the result of years of indoctrination, a bill to be paid along with Standard Oil, Master Charge, and the telephone company.

It wasn't a whole lot of fun, we finally admitted. We could hardly be classified as "cheerful givers." We were conscientiously doing our religious duty, and that was about it.

But we began noticing what the New Testament said about giving. And we began thinking about the word *giving* itself. Giving — the Christmas/birthday kind — was a neat experience. It was a joyful, even emotional exchange. It generated lots of smiles.

So Grace and I decided to play a little semantic game with ourselves. We declared a revolt against any further tithing. "We quit!" we said. "Instead, we're going to begin giving to the Lord. We're going to think of it as giving, and we're going to enjoy it."

We set a minimum size for our gifts of 10 percent of each paycheck. We decided we didn't ever want to go lower than that, but would go higher whenever we wanted to.

To make us remember, we established a routine of praying together over the Lord's check each time, usually at Sunday morning breakfast. The envelope would be sitting there between the salt and pepper shakers, and we'd say, "Lord, here's a gift for you. We're going to put it in the offering at church this morning, and we want you to know how much we appreciate you."

You may think this is foolishness, but I can tell you that it has totally changed our feelings about giving. We think it's put things into proper perspective.

We're currently away from the 10 percent figure altogether. We've set a different percentage and, with the aid of the handy calculator, it's just as easy to compute every time we plan a new budget.

However you choose to figure it, give the Lord the first slice out of the pie. And smile when you do it.

Groceries, gasoline, and garbage

If you're a budgeting pro, feel free to skip this section. But if you're often coming up short or finding yourself in a financial squeeze, keep going.

Certain expenses are rather unavoidable:

You have to live in some kind of housing.

You're probably making a car payment.

You're probably paying one or more insurance premiums.

You have to heat/cool your home, pay for electricity, water, garbage pick-up, and a telephone.

And you're stashing something away in savings and/or investments. (You aren't? Well, you've heard lots of sermons about how it never gets easier to save, so do it now, and make it an automatic thing. Take heed.)

You may need to be stockpiling for some taxes, if these aren't already withheld from your check.

Somebody in the family may be requiring tuition.

And you may have some loans to keep whittling away.

All these are what the accountants call *fixed expenses*. Once you've committed yourself, there's not a whole lot you can do about them. They're the same amount every month (except for heating bills, for which you need to find an average, and long-distance phone calls, for which you need to set a quota).

Write down each of these figures. They form a big block of your disbursements.

The remaining money goes toward *flexible expenses:* groceries, home furnishings, home maintenance, restaurants, clothing, laundry and dry cleaning, gas and oil, car repair, tolls, parking, fares, haircuts, trips to the beauty shop, drugstore items, postage, magazines, books, records and tapes, "nights out," sports, baby-sitters, doctors, dentists, prescriptions, gifts, and general messing around — wow! Hopefully you won't have too many more categories than those.

What's the tab for all of that?

If you haven't kept records up to now, you don't really know. You're going to have to make some educated guesses. Your guesses can be greatly improved six or even three months down the road if you head now for the nearest stationery store and pick up a family expense record booklet. They cost less than two dollars. My favorite is the kind put out by the Ideal System Company, but you choose your own.

The more accurate records you keep, the better you can see your spending patterns. And the more accurate your budget planning can become.

Now comes the fun of adding up your expenditures — your gifts to the Lord, your fixed expenses, and your flexible expenses — and seeing how far you've exceeded your monthly income! It is at this point that you *cannot* afford to throw up your hands and say, "Oh, well, it'll work out somehow." No, it won't. In fact, things will work out a little worse than you've projected, because you've no doubt forgotten some routine expenditures. And some unexpected surprises will be hitting you — perhaps a major illness, or a valve job on your car. You have no choice but to cut expenses down to your income or a little below. If God has given you $900 of take-home pay a month, it is simply wrong to keep cruising at a $1,000 or $1,100 life style. Make the budget balance, no matter how painful.

Actually, a good feeling comes over you when you've marked out a place for every dollar and when every dollar's in its place. You get rid of that vague uneasiness about whether to spend or not. You *know* whether you can afford an item or event. Some of the best feelings I've had have been taking Grace out to dinner, even when some other column of our budget was in excruciating pain. We had allocated a certain amount of money for restaurant dining, and we could go ahead and enjoy it regardless.

You are not finished with budgeting until both you and your wife can look at the figures and say, "That's good. I'm committed to making that plan work." So long as either of you have reservations about the wisdom or the equity of the various allocations, keep talking. Keep figuring. Keep adjusting. Eventually, copy it onto a clean sheet of paper, and keep it where you both can refer to it as often as necessary.

How to obey a budget

Right away, you have a couple of procedural matters to care for. How are you going to implement your budget on a daily basis? You obviously can't keep mental track of how much has been spent for what. You and your wife must look each other in the eye and solemnly swear that you'll both begin using the expense record booklet mentioned earlier. That way, for the first time in your life you'll have an answer to the periodic wail, "How come we're broke?!" It's right there in black and white.

The discipline of writing down what you spend has a couple of other benefits. It makes you face each expenditure twice — the moment when you shell out the cash, and the moment when you record it in the book. Grace and I have found that this acts as a subtle brake on our spending. (One time we decided we were tired of writing; we were mature adults now, and we didn't need to be so picky-picky. Within *four months*, we were in a serious financial hole, unable to tell how or why we'd gotten there — and eager to get back to record-keeping.)

The other benefit of this procedure is that it partially

solves the classic question of who shall be the family bookkeeper. If one person is charged with *all* the paperwork, it can get to be a grind as well as an irritant trying to keep track of what the other person is spending. But if the expense record book is always in a handy location — the kitchen, for example — and both you and your wife are constantly jotting down cash outlays, neither of you has to play the role of cross-examiner.

Naturally, somebody has to write the checks every payday. I don't know that it makes a great deal of difference whether it's you or your wife, assuming you both know how to add, subtract, and spell. Whichever of you takes on this responsibility is merely following through on the *jointly* planned budget anyway. So it's no great position of power and glory. Whenever there's not enough to cover the bills due, and hence some bills have to be postponed, the two of you can together decide which ones.

The family check-writer also has the responsibility of keeping the bills and other financial papers organized. Many households have gotten in trouble simply because their payables were scattered in three different rooms of the house. A few years ago my ingenious mother gave me an odd but wonderful Christmas gift: a nicely repainted metal lunchbucket, not for lunches but for household records. It has cardboard dividers inside for "Bills Due," "Charge Slips Waiting," "Bills Paid," "Paycheck Stubs," "Checking Account Statements," and a couple of other things. The checkbook rests in front. It's fantastic! In case of a fire, Grace and I would probably grab our kids and that lunchbucket ahead of anything else, because it has everything we ever want to know about our budget.

Which items are paid by check and which in cash? (Your decision may depend on whether or not you're charged for each check you write.) Here's one workable breakdown:

Checks	Cash
The Lord	Groceries
House mortgage or rent	Home supplies
Utilities	Restaurants
Insurance premiums	Clothing
Car payments	Laundry/dry cleaning
Savings	Tolls, parking
Gas, oil, repairs (through charge cards)	Barber, beauty shop
	Drugstore Items
Tuition	Miscellaneous
Subscriptions, books, and records (some through charge cards)	Postage
	"Special events," baby-sitting
	Gifts
Medical	

The check items, as you can see, are a mixture of fixed and flexible expenses. That makes it nice, in that the checking money becomes a sort of pool in which the big bills and little bills can slosh back and forth. If there's a big car repair bill one month, the medical bills can be postponed slightly, and vice versa. This takes place without bothering the day-to-day activity in the cash columns.

I've deliberately arranged for the car and life insurance premiums to come due at the end of the year, when there's a Christmas bonus to cover them. That way they don't play havoc with our month-to-month flow. If you're "richer" at certain times of the year, you might consider jockeying your annual and semiannual bills toward those times.

When it comes to cash, Grace is responsible for certain funds, such as groceries, while I'm responsible for others, such as restaurants. You're going to laugh at this, but I'll tell you anyway: We've even gone so far as to set some of the funds aside in separate little plastic boxes so we *know* whether there's any cash in that fund or not. "Clothing" is one of these; "nights out" is another. We've found that we simply can't trust ourselves to keep either of these in line without an actual, visible "kitty." If the greenbacks are there, okay; if they aren't, we don't spend.

This reflects a basic premise of sound financial operation: *Don't spend it until you've got it. Don't jump the gun.* We laugh at little children who bounce up and down and say they can't wait until Christmas; we discipline them for sneaking cookies a half-hour before dinner. Yet we are sometimes just as guilty when it comes to money. We *just can't wait* until we actually have the money in hand. We can see it coming toward us, and so we go ahead and spend early. Before long, we're going ahead and spending without asking whether the money is soon to come or not — and down that road lies big trouble.

The most enticing form of jumping the gun, of course, is the charge card. I've proven to myself over the years that I can use the convenience of charging gasoline without torpedoing the budget. The monthly total is fairly constant, and there's not much temptation to splurge in this particular area. But we would never put a fund like clothing on a charge basis. The result, we know from experience, would be swift disaster.

Charge cards facilitate the store manager's dream: impulse buying. And impulse buying is what ruins the well-laid plans of a budget. Hence, another rule of sound finances: *When in doubt — wait.* You may miss an occasional hot deal, but it's worth it. Grace and I are still growling about the encyclopedia salesman whose special price was available *only that week* back in 1970. We told ourselves Vickie needed encyclopedias for school (false). We told ourselves all kinds of things as we took the plunge, withdrawing a life insurance dividend to pay for the set.

By the time Nathan and the twins will be old enough to use them, they'll be ten years out of date. The rotten part is that I *knew* that evening we didn't really need a set of encyclopedias right then; I just couldn't muster the courage to tell the guy no and would he please get out of my living room.

A bargain is not a bargain unless you need it.

Of all the areas of a budget that call for maturity on the part of the husband, the greatest is the car. In most households, car expenses are to the husband what groceries are to the wife: a major category about which one spouse knows quite a lot and the other knows next to nothing. You can walk in the door after paying a $78 repair bill, lay three or four sentences of mechanical jargon on her — and she's helpless. She doesn't know what you're talking about, let alone whether the repair was essential or not.

But she does know that you just dropped another $78 on the car. And that hurts, no matter how unavoidable it was.

Our household records show that for the past three years I have sunk 16 percent of the family fortune each year into automobiles — gas, oil, repairs, payments, insurance, license plates, and municipal vehicle taxes. In the same period, Grace has shelled out no higher than 13 percent for groceries. These two categories, along with housing and our gifts to the Lord, make up the Big Four of our budget. Everything else is minor by comparison.

I have a responsibility to Grace and the children to hold the automobile area in line, even though they don't have the mechanical know-how to question my decisions. This means choosing dependable cars in the first place, finding honest and competent repairmen (which can be quite a trick sometimes), and changing oil and getting lube jobs on schedule.

In my case, I have come to believe that it means something even more basic — and more sizable in terms of dollars. It means controlling my attitude toward cars in general, viewing them as the pieces of machinery they are rather than extensions of my own ego or self-image. It means resisting Detroit's media blitzes every fall that tempt me to trade for the newest, biggest, and best. It means getting rid of the myth that cars are an investment. They are *not;* they do *not* appreciate in value or pay returns on the initial capital. They *cost* money — lots of it. Some of them can be resold for more than others, but never for the full amount of what you've spent on them.

Like most men, I remember with considerable sentiment my first car during high-school days: a black 1950 Mercury coupe. I paid $100 for it. My self-image was tremendously bound up in that car . . . those rear-wheel covers . . . the deep-throated rumble that turned heads in the school parking lot . . . well, you know what I mean.

Next came a long black '48 Dodge limo I bought from a funeral director for whom I worked one summer; it was a campus conversation piece that fall. But its charm was soon lost, and in its place came a flashy '56 Olds Holiday two-door hardtop (with a cracked head, I might add, and poorly patched rocker panels that disintegrated in the salted streets of the first Chicago winter). No matter. I was a taller-than-average guy who needed a big car, right? Next, a pink '56 Cadillac Coupe de Ville, followed by a '63 Mercury Monterey with that classy reverse-slant window in the back.

Suddenly, I realized something: I was spending an awful lot of money on cars, and there was no end in sight. It took a while, but Grace and I finally came to the conclusion that what we needed was a basic means of transportation, not a status symbol. We dumped the ailing Mercury for a used Volvo and drove it for the next 6½ years.

I remember the first year I didn't go to drool and dream

at the Chicago Auto Show. It was like giving up an old friend. But I decided I'd be better off without the bombardment. I haven't been back since.

Not that there's anything immoral about an auto show. I'm just saying that for me, it was my annual orgy of automobile covetousness, and I eventually had to deal with that problem, for my own sake as well as for my family's.

How to revise a budget

Obviously, every time you get a raise you need a new budget. But there are other reasons as well. Perhaps your expenses change — a son or daughter starts college, for example. Perhaps your long-range goals change. There was a point early in our marriage at which Grace and I decided to stop using her teaching pay for stereo components and bedroom suites and start socking it away toward a down payment on a house. We knew we'd eventually be living on one income instead of two, so why not now?

Again, we had to trick ourselves into it. We dubbed the salad days of the past the Era of Elasticity. Now we were beginning the Era of Rigidity. (To tell you the truth, I think we've been in Rigidity ever since.) Our goals had changed, and we restructured our spending patterns to match.

The other time when a budget needs revision is when it's just not working. You haven't allocated enough money for utilities, or gifts, or nights out, and you're getting thoroughly frustrated. It's not that you're unwilling to abide by the budget; it's just that the thing is out of whack. Okay; change it. Face the problem. Don't go on gnashing your teeth. Shift some dollars from one of the other accounts. Or find a way to raise income. Naturally, you have to keep the bottom line in balance whatever you do, but if you're in an intolerable situation, sit down with your wife and take a good, hard look at your priorities as expressed by your budget.

What to do when the budget's been blown

For all your care and discipline, there will be times when you — or she — will simply blow it. You'll misplace a $20 bill somewhere. You'll get a traffic ticket. A repair service will rip you off. You'll succumb to the allure of a new sport coat and whip out a charge card before you think.

Well, it's not the end of the world. After all, some things in life are more important than money. Confession, for example. It's *her* money that's been squandered as well as yours, remember? So don't keep her in the dark. Tell her what happened, and how you feel about it . . . and don't be surprised if the whole ordeal draws the two of you closer to each other. You may face a tough month or two recovering from the financial loss, but you'll face it together, and out of such ordeals comes the deepening of love and trust.

The Scriptures direct "those who are rich in this present world [e.g., the majority of us North Americans, compared to the rest of the world] not to be arrogant nor to put their hope in wealth, which is so uncertain, but to put their hope in God, who richly provides us with everything for our enjoyment" (1 Tim. 6:17).

Your household and mine need a leader with that kind of attitude.

[1]Mike McGrady, *The Kitchen Sink Papers* (Garden City, N.Y.: Doubleday, 1975), pp. 26, 27.

5

A Master,
a Mistress,
and Two Slaves

5

A Master, a Mistress, and Two Slaves

Having dealt with the shortage of money, we turn now to the remaining two shortages, time and energy. They too can breed considerable tension.

Time and energy are gifts from God just as money is. Especially *discretionary* time and energy — the leftovers after we've finished working, sleeping, and eating. The question may again be posed:

What shall *we* (husband and wife) do with *our* time and energy?

Sounds pretty wide-open, doesn't it? But the fact is that society and tradition have rather thoroughly programed us with a set of answers. Husbands do certain things around the house. Wives do certain things around the house. Each has his/her "place."

How valid are the traditions we've been handed? Before you read on, find a pencil and mark this check list according to the actual nature of each task, not according to what happens to be the usual at your house.

	Basically a husband's job	Basically a wife's job	Doesn't really matter
1. Opening pickle jars	☐	☐	☐
2. Having babies	☐	☐	☐
3. Changing the car's oil	☐	☐	☐
4. Changing the baby's diapers	☐	☐	☐
5. Mowing the yard	☐	☐	☐
6. Vacuuming the carpet	☐	☐	☐
7. Waxing the car	☐	☐	☐
8. Waxing the kitchen floor	☐	☐	☐
9. Painting a ceiling	☐	☐	☐
10. Getting kids to bed	☐	☐	☐

Women's Liberation, of course, has forced all of us to think twice about these things. It's had the net effect of moving more and more items into the "doesn't really matter" column.

Tasks related to basic anatomy, of course (such as numbers 1 and 2 on the list), are not going to get bumped around. In terms of brute physical strength, men are estimated to be 50 percent stronger than women, and that's simply not going to change. Women, on the other hand, have been found to have a somewhat greater tolerance for extreme heat.

But when it comes to the overwhelming majority of tasks that really have nothing to do with anatomy, a lot of things are up for grabs. Some of us are cheering the current reassessment. Others of us are disturbed by it. Some of us are worried that the ultimate goal is to completely obliterate *la différence,* to create a unisex world. Many of us are confused about the new definitions of masculinity and femininity and whether they're improvements or setbacks.

And while we're philosophizing about the state of the culture at large, we're overlooking the nearest and most relevant situation: our own households. It's much easier to critique Barbara Walters as a TV news anchorperson or to expound the merits and flaws of the Equal Rights Amendment than it is to look at what's happening under our own roof.

We might as well face it: it takes a fair chunk of work to run a house. Work on the outside that brings in a paycheck, yes, but also work right there on the premises. And it's not all fun work. A certain percentage of it is outright drudgery. Servant-type work.

Who's going to do it?

Tradition says, "If it's anything to do with the kitchen, laundry room, bathroom, bedroom, or living areas — the wife. If it's anything to do with the garage, basement, or yard — the husband."

Now you may have altered that tradition to a greater or lesser degree. You and your wife may not have come to the marriage in the first place with identical traditions. Grace's father, a minister and former denominational executive, happens also to be a rather happy vacuumer as well as grocery shopper. I don't remember my dad doing either, unless it was a special occasion. So I naturally don't think about volunteering to vacuum or go to the supermarket — which sometimes, even after eleven years, Grace still finds herself expecting more or less from habit.

But these are minor wrinkles in the overall pattern of traditional husband and wife roles. None of us are free from them. And if someone were to follow any of our wives around with a stopwatch, chances are she'd pile up a greater number of drudgery minutes than we could any week of the year.

Mike McGrady, the newspaperman mentioned in the

last chapter who traded places with his wife for a year, realized this rather powerfully one night as he stood ironing clothes while his kids watched TV.

> I have known little in life more depressing than that experience, standing there ironing my daughter's massive wardrobe, listening to Bob Hope and actor Burt Reynolds trading tacky little jokes about the actor's affair with an older woman.
>
> On second thought, it might have seemed as depressing without the television set on. Any job requiring the constant repetition of a simple act is going to seem dumb. No assembly-line worker in Detroit, no person tightening the same bolt on the same door of every sedan coming out of a factory, ever put in more dummy time than a normal house-wife.[1]

Granted, life at McGrady's old newspaper office had not always been a lark. There had been cranky people and unreliable machinery and all of the normal irritants of any job. But there had also been some significant and applaudable goals in spite of the obstacles. It had its rewards.

Mike's wife Corinne was a person of considerable talent. Nevertheless, from almost the beginning of the marriage, Corinne had

> played Female. That is to say, she stayed home with the children and did the cleaning and cooking. It is, in retrospect, incredible that she did all this routinely and without complaint. . . .
>
> And since she was an artist, since she was gifted and creative, she not unnaturally attempted to apply her skills to her new life as housewife. It was a little like asking a nuclear physicist to apply his talents to sweeping public streets. She did well at the most mundane tasks, very well indeed, but who can measure the toll? Not just the toll in years — for these could have been her most productive

years — but a toll in spirit. There were rough
times, times when in the middle of the night she
would flee family and house, get in the car and
drive for hours along shore roads. There were other
times when her patience would be worn thin as
gauze and that normally well-modulated voice
turned into something out of a low-budget horror
movie.[2]

It was out of a desire to change some of that that the
McGrady experiment was born.

The question for us husbands is not whether our wives
are willing to be the servants of the household. The
question is, *are we?* Here is one of the places where the
high-flying concepts of chapter 2 hit the road. *Do we
really want to be servants in our own homes on a day-to-
day basis?* There is a certain irreducible amount of work
to a household, requiring a certain amount of human time
and human energy, modern conveniences notwithstanding. Whose time and energy shall be expended to do the
work?

If you are committed to the idea of one common life,
and if you are determined before God to be the
leader/servant of that common life, then you face the
practical need to take your place along with your wife
(and your children, as they're able) in doing the work.
The fun work. The drudgery. The so-so kind of work. You
also share in the enjoyment of leisure time when the
work's done. Whatever's happening, whatever is to be
endured or enjoyed, you're in it together.

Here are some specifics to remember:

She's not dumb

Your wife has a brain. She spent a number of years in
school cultivating her mind. She's lived approximately as
long as you have — maybe longer. She's no dumb kid.

And her mind is probably as flexible and as capable of adapting to various challenges as yours is. It is never very smart to assume that she couldn't understand or comprehend this or that.

Harold and Jeanette Myra are close friends of ours; he and I worked together for several years at *Campus Life* magazine. One January night the four of us were at their place. The temperature hadn't gotten above zero all day. I can't remember the details, but for some reason one of their cars had been left sitting outdoors in a parking lot since the day before, and Jeanette said, "Would you two mind dropping me off on your way home so I can pick up the car and bring it back here?"

"Fine," I said. Then I made a terrible mistake. I temporarily forgot that Jeanette was a farmer's daughter from Wisconsin. "But don't you want Harold to come along to get it started?" I asked.

She looked at me as if I'd just questioned her ability to make a decent pot of coffee.

"Why do I need Harold?" she shot back. "If I can't start it, he sure can't start it!"

Harold duly agreed with that, I duly apologized, and we drove her to the dark, icy parking lot. She hopped in the car, turned the key, kicked the accelerator the way it needed to be kicked, and started the engine on the first try just like it was her father's old John Deere.

There's no biological reason why women shouldn't be allowed to touch the mechanical side of life. There's no reason of any kind to shield wives from the higher disciplines of the mind: politics, economics, law, theology, mass communication, international affairs, and the other supposedly masculine domains. Indeed, to do so is criminal. It is a denial of divine gifts and aptitudes.

You're not privileged

So long as there are certain understandings, spoken or unspoken, that you are "above" having to do certain grundy jobs, you are not a servant. It's sometimes hard to realize where the pockets of privilege still lie. The traditions are so strong. They may never come out into the open unless you get up the courage to ask your wife directly, "Are there some things that you 'just know' not to ask me to do? In what ways am I still playing the role of the big cheese without realizing it?" She'll tell you!

I think every father who's ever changed a diaper can remember his first clumsy attempt. I recall thinking that somebody sure botched the engineering design along the way; how was that big, square piece of cloth supposed to fit this little, tiny, rounded bottom?

And, of course, the smell and the mess are not exactly pleasant. Especially at the beginning, when you're getting used to it.

But since when is a grown man afraid to get his hands dirty? That's the first thing you learn on your first after-school job as a teen-ager — sometimes you just have to get in there and do the job and clean up later. I will always remember a particular chicken coop on a certain widow's farm four miles north of Whitewater, Kansas, where I as a high school sophomore learned that lesson. We'd just moved into the community, and this woman offered me half a Saturday's work using a pitchfork and shovel on about a ten-inch layer of manure. Well, I survived. You can probably tell a similar tale yourself.

So what's so bad about diapers?

After the twins arrived (180 diapers a week to start), I even did something about the engineering problem. Grace was gone for several hours, and I said to myself, *There's got to be a better way*. So I put my masculine mind to work and figured out a tighter way to fold and pin.

I realize that not all my readers have kids, and many of you who do are past the diaper stage. I'm just using this as an illustration of the servanthood motif in a very practical area for husbands.

Find a need and fill it

The more we reexamine our male and female roles in Western society and the more we question the old stereotypes, the more we have to face the necessity for a new order. Some couples engage in writing marriage contracts, in which they spell out precisely who shall pay for what and who shall be responsible for the less exciting parts of running a household. It's all there in black and white. The contracts are rewritten from time to time as needs and feelings change.

Such an approach is probably an improvement over the old silent assumptions — but I think we Christians can do even better. We can, if we really want to, create a miniature of God's kingdom of love right here and now in our own homes. Instead of worrying about the protection of egos, instead of searching for the perfectly just and equitable division of labor, instead of safeguarding against infringement of rights — we can surrender our rights and our lives to each other. This results in a *flow* of service unhindered by union rules; both husband and wife jump in and do whatever needs to be done at the moment. If a child's nose needs to be wiped or a flower patch needs to be weeded, either spouse responds without reference to a contracted list of duties.

There are times — not as many as I would like — when I sense Grace and myself flowing as a work team in an effective and strangely rewarding way. Walking in from an evening church service with three cranky children who need to get to bed, we both sort of spring into action.

There's almost no conversation between us; we know the fifty-nine things that need to be done, and in what order, and we go at it. About twenty minutes later, when all three are down and the lights have been turned off, we meet each other in the hall, sigh, and usually say something inane like, "Hello — how are you?" Our work is done — notice, *our* work — and now we're ready to enjoy some adult time together.

I don't mean to imply that all things can be handled by instinct. Some parts of household life are complicated enough — menu planning, for example — that an administrator is needed. Somebody has to accept it as a responsibility and follow through more or less by himself or herself. But there are probably not as many of these as we think. The sensitive husband and wife can in most areas develop a synergistic approach that lightens the load and deepens the love of both.

As Ambrose Bierce, an American journalist of three generations ago, said, "Marriage is a community consisting of a master, a mistress, and two slaves, making in all, two."

[1]Mike McGrady, *The Kitchen Sink Papers* (Garden City, N.Y.: Doubleday, 1975), p. 82.
[2]Ibid., pp. 30, 31.

6

It's
a Job

6

It's
a Job

This is not a book about how to succeed in business, with or without really trying. That is a science all its own.

But it's impossible to talk about the job of being a husband without taking into account our occupations. After all, work consumes half or more of our waking hours, if we add the work we sometimes bring home at night and the miscellaneous time we spend thinking about work problems.

That constitutes a rather major chunk of our lives. No wonder we men are more often identified and categorized by occupation than any other kind of label. In social situations we make small talk with each other by asking, "And what do you do?" We expect the guy to say, "I'm an electrician (or state senator, or supermarket manager, or whatever)." We would be rather surprised if he said instead, "I'm an avid reader," or "I'm a Little League coach," or "I'm a husband."

There are some good reasons why work predominates,

of course. (1) We like to eat. (2) We've been programed since childhood to grow up and be gainfully employed. (3) What else is there to do all day? Working for money is one of the presuppositions about what a husband does; it's part of our responsibility. Even the Scripture says, "If anyone does not provide . . . especially for his immediate family, he has denied the faith and is worse than an unbeliever" (1 Tim. 5:8).

A lot of us work for an additional reason: the challenge of it. We've been fortunate enough to find our way into an occupation that we find intriguing, that pits us against a set of obstacles, that dares us to wage battle and overcome. The proof of success may be any number of things — the year-end profit on the bottom line, or the number of students whom we successfully prepare for the next level of education, or the score on the stadium scoreboard at the end of the game. We find it psychologically rewarding to see what we can achieve, aside from the pay.

Not all of us, however, are in a challenging job. Some of us are bored to death. Either there's no place to go in our chosen field, or we're not qualified for a promotion or change. The only reward is the paycheck. Management people know that such a situation is not the best for either the worker or the company, and in many cases they are trying to adjust things, to instill some challenge into the work, whether in the form of bonuses for extra output or by rewriting job descriptions.

Even a boring job, of course, is usually preferable to no job at all. Some of us know the anxiety and inner pain of being unemployed. Men in this situation are the most keenly aware of the centrality of work in a man's life.

Our wives are venturing into the world of work in ever increasing numbers and are facing the same challenges (or lack thereof). Either to gain a higher standard of living for the family or to diversify their lives, or both, women are on the payroll.

The question each couple has to face is whether, in the long run, the household is helped or hurt by this. There is no question that the New Testament instructs wives to "guide the house" (1 Tim. 5:14 KJV) and to be "keepers at home" (Titus 2:5 KJV). But it's also rather obvious that if there are no children, or the children are in school throughout the day, most women can do an adequate job of guiding the house and still have a number of hours left over each week, thanks in part to modern conveniences. The use of that leftover time is a matter of Christian stewardship, and the Lord is obviously happier with a wife who uses those hours for productive wage-earning or volunteer ministry than for deadening her mind with soap operas at home.

Whether the wife is employed or not, work is undoubtedly the biggest thing we do *apart* from each other. No other item on our schedule pulls us away from each other for such long stretches of time. Work therefore has the capacity to drive a giant wedge between us. By its very nature it leads to two separate lives instead of one common one. Thus, it is important for us to consider how work can harmonize with a marriage and, specifically, with our role as husbands.

Containing the camel

Most of us push pretty hard at our jobs. We know it's a competitive world out there, and if we don't produce, there are lots of other guys just waiting for the chance to replace us. Part of the genius of free-enterprise capitalism is its ability to motivate, to crank us up, to draw from us the last full measure of energy and devotion.

Some of us push so hard that the job, in a curious sort of way, *becomes* us. We are the job, and it is us. If we meet our sales projection, we see ourselves not only as successful salesmen but as successful and worthwhile persons. If we don't make it, we're flops, and not just in the occupational sense. We *ourselves* are plagued with feelings of failure.

These are powerful feelings, and there's no way to shut them off when we come home. The genius of capitalism thus becomes a great danger as well, in that the rush of competition obscures the fact that we are human beings, made in the image of God, worthwhile in and of ourselves whether we make the sales projection or not. We are still, among other things, husbands who have been gifted with wives and households that need us — not just our money, but *us*.

I remember a bull session one night a few years ago with seven other editors. We were talking about the priority of our work. We were all young, bright-eyed, ambitious types, eager to prove ourselves to our bosses and our readers and to continue to climb to greater responsibility and prestige.

We lectured each other on how leadership and excellence demands sacrifice, about how we had to rid ourselves of the clock mentality and commit ourselves to doing the job, whether it required forty hours or seventy. "Anybody who's not willing to make a total commitment to this thing, to go all out," it was said, "is just not going to come up with the award winners. Anything less means mediocrity for the product, and it also means putting a lid on one's own advancement."

It was at about this point that a couple of us began asking, "Yeah, but what about the other parts of one's life — you know, those incidental things out on the periphery, like wife, kids, church, neighbors, physical fitness? Don't they get at least a little piece of the action?"

No one exactly mounted an attack against these, but the drift persisted heavily in favor of work being paramount. As the evening wore on, I found myself increasingly in the role of odd man out as I tried to defend the validity of turning off editing and turning on some other things at certain points of the week. I wasn't really clear in my own mind, but I kept fumbling around saying things like, "Look, I'm committed to excellence. I want to be the best editor in the field. But I'm not sure I have to dismiss everything else from my frame of consciousness in order to reach that goal."

That was in June. By the next January, three of the people at that jam session had resigned their positions and altered their life styles dramatically. One of the three stopped by my office a couple of months later to say, "Hey, remember that night when we were all talking about commitment to the job and how important it was?"

"Yeah, I remember."

He shook his head with a grin. "That sure was a bunch of garbage."

Not everyone would agree with his assessment, but more and more businessmen and managers of all kinds are coming to understand that it is neither smart nor possible to try to *own* people. President Carter demonstrated this in one of his first cabinet meetings when he stated that he didn't want any marriages breaking up because of loyalty to himself.

Our jobs are somewhat like the proverbial camel asking to warm its nose inside the Arab's tent. There's nothing wrong with being nice to camels, but they don't make good house guests. A job that is allowed to take over the entire life of a family is a job out of control.

And if it eventually wrecks the tent, everybody's out in the cold, including the camel. What has been gained? Many of us have known super-achievers on the job whose personal lives were such a shambles that eventually even their careers were destroyed.

But I'm not that bad, you say. *I'm not a workaholic.*

The truth of that claim may depend in part upon your way of thinking about your schedule. Do you have a priority list in your head? Have you said to yourself, "X is the number one priority as far as I'm concerned; Y is number two; Z is number three," and so forth?

If you function on that basis, you have created some built-in problems. (1) You've set up your wife as the opponent of your job, your church as the opponent of your wife, etc. Each is competing for as high a placement as possible, and when one wins, the other loses. (2) The items at the bottom of the list don't stand a chance. There will never be enough time to get to them.

An alternate approach is to state that there are *a number* of important "top-priority" items in your life, and each gets a share. Not long ago I sat down and wrote out a weekly time budget. I had no idea how many of the 168 hours of my week I could account for, but I thought it would be fun to try.

I came up with the following categories. You may want to use them for your own analysis.

	Hours per week	% of total
CHURCH		
Regular meetings	____	
Other groups, committees, boards, etc.	____	
Travel time	____	
Preparation for teaching, music, etc.	____	
Subtotal	____	____

	Hours per week	% of total
PHYSICAL		
Sleep	_____	
Meals	_____	
Dressing, shaving, etc.	_____	
Exercise, sports	_____	
Subtotal	_____	_____
WORK		
On-the-job time	_____	
Travel time	_____	
Extra work at home	_____	
Subtotal	_____	_____
FAMILY		
Wife communication (home as well as "out")	_____	
Children time	_____	
Parents and in-laws	_____	
Budgeting, bookkeeping, bill-paying	_____	
House maintenance	_____	
Yard maintenance/ snow removal	_____	
Auto maintenance	_____	
Subtotal	_____	_____
SELF		
Devotional life	_____	
Reading	_____	
TV	_____	
Subtotal	_____	_____
COMMUNITY INVOLVEMENT	_____	_____

I was amazed that I could actually account for 165 hours. That told me that my schedule is more packed than I thought, that there's not much time for general loafing. (If you're wondering how this book ever got written, the answer is vacation time!)

But this little exercise enabled me to look at the percentages and ask myself: Is my week in balance? Am I giving the right amount of hours to each of these areas? Am I being a responsible steward of God's gift of time?

As with money, we often fail to get the big picture. We are taken up with individual trees instead of the forest.

And work is a very aggressive species; it can spread and choke out some of the less sturdy trees that also deserve a place in the sun.

Some special dilemmas

The tradesman whose work is carefully governed by the clock and union rules does not face as many time decisions as the executive, the self-employed businessman, or the professional. Those who are judged not by numbers of hours but by intangibles are the ones who fight with the camel most often.

The problem is especially acute for people in the ministry. Here the motivation is not so much financial as theological. What can be more important than doing the work of God? There are billions of people who haven't heard a decent presentation of the gospel . . . there are swarms of needy, confused, and/or questioning people right at the doorstep . . . how can a pastor or missionary take time even for a cup of coffee with his wife?

For most clergy, the breakdown of activities on pages 92 and 93 has to be altered, since church and work are synonymous. And it's deadly serious work. A guy can turn off the lights and lock the doors of his hot-dog stand and know that the world won't suffer greatly without his services. Even an insurance salesman or a university professor knows that his work is not totally indispensable.

But what if a potential suicide can't get through to the minister? Doctors can at least relax in the knowledge that their patients can always head for the local hospital. The pastor, in contrast, is often the one and only source of help in some extreme situations.

There is no denying that all of this drives ministers, missionaries, church executives, and other clergy to unhealthy and even dangerous life styles. The toll is often most apparent in their wives and children. They find themselves with all kinds of feelings of resentment, isolation, and disillusionment not only against the man of the house, but against the God and the institution he serves. This immediately triggers guilt feelings: *How terrible of me to want him home when he's out serving the Lord.*

So the wife keeps quiet. I know of one man who in the earlier years of his ministry kept such a schedule that he found himself out of town during the births of each of his three children. I am glad to report that more recently he's come to see (and preach to his colleagues) that it makes no sense to try to build the kingdom of God at the expense of another, even more basic divine institution: the home. The Scriptures give no basis for such madness. In fact, among the qualifications for overseers in 1 Timothy 3 is the following: "He must manage his own family well and see that his children obey him with proper respect. (If anyone does not know how to manage his own family, how can he take care of God's church?)" (vv. 4,5).

That . . . takes time. There is no way a minister can put in fourteen-hour days seven days a week and do any kind of a job of leading/serving his own household. It's impossible.

It takes discipline for such a person to apportion his time responsibly. It's all the harder because the work of the church is, among other things, a nights-and-weekends situation. That's when people are available for appointments, classes, committee meetings, and public worship services. The pastorate is actually a swing-shift job! So when does that leave for fixing leaky faucets and taking one's wife shopping? Somehow, it doesn't feel right doing those things on Tuesday mornings when the rest of the world is hard at work. But why not?

The peculiar nature of the ministry calls for some peculiar and rather forceful solutions. I remember seeing one church calendar that included, along with the Sunday school sessions and choir rehearsals and women's groups, a notation of "Pastor's Day Off" each week. Just in case the members forget . . . or are so dense as to assume that Sunday is *his* day of rest . . . it's right there on the calendar in black and white for them to read.

In search of sanity

It's a shame, in a way, that for most of us, work has to be sealed in an airtight set of hours with no allowances for family. There's a lot to be said for the work schedule of such countries as Italy, Spain, and Portugal, where people start early and work straight through to 1:00 P.M. — and then go home for a leisurely lunch and siesta. The shops and offices open up again at 5:00 P.M. for another three-hour stretch.

Granted, the cities are smaller, and commuting time is not so great. But we Americans would do well to consider how we might blend work and family life through some creative scheduling. One of the beautiful assets of farming is that it offers so many tasks that family members can do *together*.

Dr. Charlie Shedd, in his book *Smart Dads I Know*, tells about one bank president who decided to stop doing evening business with out-of-town guests in fancy restaurants. Instead, he began inviting them home for hamburgers around the pool with his wife and kids. "At first I wondered if it would hurt my business," he says. "Funny — things actually went better. As a matter of fact, I've made some awfully big deals by this pool over the hamburgers."

Another man, a small-town doctor, told his two sons that whenever they needed him, they could come and rap three times on the back door of his office, and he'd be there. It's interesting that one of those sons grew up to be Dr. Eugene Nida, executive secretary of the American Bible Society.

A third father faced the tough job of raising his daughter by himself. She remembers one very special thing about those years:

> When I started to school, my father gave me ten cents, and . . . he said, "Patty, I want you always to keep this dime in your purse. Any time you need me, you call me at the plant. Tell them you want to talk to your dad, and I guarantee they'll let you right through." There is no way I could tell you what that ten cent piece from my father meant. Even when I didn't need him, just to know I had it in my purse made me feel secure. [1]

Actually, there are a lot of little things that all of us can do to give our families glimpses into our work. Plant or office tours can be fascinating for them; suddenly the places and situations we talk about at home become real. We can also arrange for our wives to meet our work associates — not only during a walk-through but in evening social situations. That way when we come home and growl, "The boss has got to be out of his mind," she's in a better position to sympathize with us!

Seriously, the more she knows about what we do, the more she can respond to this major part of our lives, the better she can brainstorm with us on ways to solve work problems, and the greater her own sense of security will be. I make it a habit to bring home issues of the company newspaper, new catalogs, company advertisements and public-relations brochures, even some of the trade journals, just so Grace can feel what I'm involved in, ask questions, and participate in my life on the job.

The containment of one's work within a proper balance is not the only occupational dilemma. We also run into problems such as stagnation, when we feel we're not growing in our work and need a change of some kind. Or our employer asks us to move into a new and different responsibility. Or a job offer from the outside comes along, and we wonder whether to switch or not.

All of these call for careful consideration, prayer, and discussion with our wives. It is important to remember, as we said before, that the work is not us; it is only something we do. To change our work is not to change our basic identity. In fact, it may even stretch the real us to a new and better shape.

Dr. Anthony Campolo, a Philadelphia professor of sociology, tells about a colleague of his who finally decided he'd had it with teaching. The daily grind of lecturing and grading papers seemed pointless to him, so he resigned his post at Trenton State College and got a job as a mailman.

His mother was understandably worried. "He's got a Ph.D.!" she told Campolo. "Why don't you go see him and try to get him straightened out?"

Dr. Campolo obliged, but didn't make much progress. The man said, "I know it's a bit strange, but I really enjoy what I'm doing far more than the classroom." All arguments to the contrary were brushed aside.

Finally, Campolo said something like, "Well, I guess that's fine, as long as one does a good job in whatever field he chooses."

"Oh, no," the man objected. "I'm a terrible mailman."

"How is that?"

"It takes me forever. Most guys are finished by one o'clock in the afternoon. I seldom get back before five."

"Why?" Campolo wondered.

"I visit!" he announced with a flourish. "You've no idea how many lonely senior citizens there are on my mail route. So I stop and talk. I must be having twenty cups of coffee a day — I can't even get to sleep at night for all the visiting I'm doing."

The man had taken some occupational risk — and found fulfillment.

Dead end

The biggest occupational change of all, of course, is the change nobody wants — the loss of a job. To be a healthy adult male who's out of work is a trauma we'd all like to avoid. But that's not always possible.

Among the never-to-be-forgotten days of my life is one hot Friday afternoon in June a few years ago when I was asked to come to the office of my supervisor. Rumors had been flying that the financial squeeze was on and that some clerical people were going to have to be cut, but nothing had been said about anyone else.

I sat there listening to an obviously uncomfortable man trying to tell me as gently as possible that certain depart ments and functions had, regrettably, been chosen for elimination in order to bring the budget into line. He began naming off the victims . . . and suddenly my years of service to the organization had come to an abrupt end.

He insisted, of course, that this was no reflection on my abilities, etc., etc., but that it was a necessary move by management to . . . I forget the rest. All I remember from there on is going out to my car, driving toward home, and pulling off to the side of the road to try and figure out how to tell Grace.

I couldn't escape the fact that no matter what he'd said about how this was solely a financial pruning — when the chips were down, I was one of the guys they could afford to get along without. There was no way to whitewash that fact. My self-esteem was crumbling fast.

Somehow now, with the perspective that comes with

the passing years, I believe that every highly charged, self-confident type like myself needs the experience of such a blow. To walk in your front door, to look at the wife who loves you, to swallow a couple of times and then say, "Well, uh, guess what — come Monday morning, I won't be going anywhere" . . . somehow, the pain of that confession cuts you down to size, confronts you with your inadequacies, humbles you, makes you vulnerable. And in your helplessness, the two of you are drawn closer together.

You find yourselves leaning on each other, praying desperately for divine help, and at the same time counting the blessings that remain. The future is terrifying, and yet at the same time you can view it as a clean slate upon which God may write all sorts of interesting things. In our case, we had to wait five weeks before I went to work again, whereas others have hung in limbo much longer. But even in that amount of time we were made deeply aware of where our truly permanent, reliable resources lay. We were not to trust in organizations or companies or employment agencies or even our own talents or "connections"; we were to rely on the God who had brought us this far and was not about to lose track of us now.

Without this confidence, a marriage can crack under the strain of joblessness. The bills mount up, and so do the questions about whether the husband is really up to the task of leadership in the family. His self-confidence is under tremendous pressure, and the longer he goes without work, the worse it gets. I found myself striving for achievement during those weeks — I dug a trench for a drain tile through the yard while I was waiting, just to demonstrate that I wasn't totally useless. But in the long run, it was the steady confidence of my wife and the knowledge that God was still in control that held the pieces together.

Whether it's the major crisis of unemployment or one of the minor bumps along the road, the sharing of our work with our wives is a tremendously helpful thing to do. She can tell when we've had a bad day, anyway, so she might as well know the specifics! Her support at such times can be beautiful.

She also deserves to know about the good times, the successes, the boss's compliments. To hold back what happens on the job, to assume that "she wouldn't understand" is to impugn her intelligence and also to retreat once again into aloneness. Even though she's not physically present for this major segment of our daily activity, she can share in both its joys and catastrophes if we give her the chance. In this way work becomes another part of the common, unified life together.

[1]Charlie Shedd, *Smart Dads I Know* (New York: Sheed and Ward, 1975), pp. 27-32.

7

The
Household
of Faith

7

The Household of Faith

The state of Illinois, where I live, has long been known for its colorful politics. The late Richard J. Daley, mayor of Chicago for twenty-one years and undisputed kingmaker of the Democratic party statewide, was perhaps the greatest but certainly not the first nor the last of our public entrepreneurs. The jokes about how Hizzoner used to win elections are legion. (The most popular: Daley and two others were on Lake Michigan in a yacht that began to sink. Since only one life buoy was available, an argument arose over who should get to use it. Finally the mayor said, "Wait a minute — let's be democratic about this instead of fighting. Let's take a vote." So each man cast his ballot, and Daley won 7-2.)

Part of the problem in Illinois, of course, is that the population is so lopsided. Seven million of the state's eleven million people are bunched together in the northeast corner (greater Chicago), while the rest are spread out on farms and in small and medium-sized communities all the way to the edge of Kentucky. The state legislature in Springfield is thus a ready-made combat zone, with the Irish, black, Polish, Jewish, and other ethnic representatives from Chicago pitted against the sturdy white Anglo-Saxon Protestants from the farm counties. The farmers don't get terribly excited about spending money to build Chicago's rapid transit system or feed its welfare mothers, while the city slickers aren't exactly turned on by the needs of the hinterlands.

With such a lack of common interests, it's not hard to see how political shenanigans arise.

The state of New York has a similar problem, with similar results. At times it has become so acute that some politicians have seriously asked whether New York City wouldn't be better off on its own as the fifty-first state of the Union. That way it wouldn't have to keep hassling with the upstate "appleknockers," as they are rather contemptuously known.

Yet one wonders whether New York City could survive alone. States are equipped to do some things that would be extremely difficult for cities to handle. And vice versa. Multilevel jurisdictions seem to be a necessity of life, in spite of the problems they cause.

It occurs to me that there's an analogy here. Just as cities and states are bound to each other but sometimes have difficulty interrelating, so do families and churches. The home and the church undeniably overlap — the same people are members of both. The church is clearly made up of husbands, wives, sons, and daughters, who obviously don't drop those identities in the narthex. Thus, the potential exists for tension between the two milieus.

But the potential also exists for common bolstering and reinforcement. In the final analysis, most of us are like New York City; we are not really interested in secession. We recognize that "unless the Lord builds the house, those who build it labor in vain" (Psalm 127 — a very family-oriented psalm, by the way). We suspect that the Lord would like to build and strengthen our various houses through the ministry of his church.

It is up to us — husbands of households as well as men of the church — to figure out how.

How the church enhances the household

The home, of course, can claim seniority as an institution. God started it at the very beginning, whereas the idea of the called-out assembly of worshipers goes back only to the time of the Exodus, around 1480 B.C. So it stands to reason that God intended this larger, more recent unit to synchronize with his smaller, more primary unit.

What is the church? It is perhaps easier to state what it is not.

• It isn't a building (although we spend major amounts of money erecting structures commonly known as churches).

• It isn't a denomination (although most denominations use the word in their formal names).

• It isn't a social arena in which we prove respectability to our friends and neighbors.

• It isn't a museum for the preservation of family tradition ("My grandfather was a Presbyterian minister, and we'll always . . .").

• It isn't a provider of free baby-sitting so you and your wife can enjoy a little peace and quiet each week.

The real essence of the church is far greater than any of these. And far more exciting. The church is meant to be a living, breathing community of Christ-followers who love and support each other to such an extent that they might be called . . .

. . . a family! A household!

At least that's what the New Testament often called it. "You are no longer foreigners and aliens," Paul wrote to the Ephesian church, "but fellow citizens with God's people and members of God's household" (2:19).

A chapter later he said, "I kneel before the Father, from whom the whole family of believers in heaven and on earth derives its name" (3:14,15).

The church is a group of people who have a great deal in common with one another because of their common Father. I ask you: what better definition of a family could there be?

The church is thus a magnification of your family and mine, with the rather clear advantage of having a Head who is far more competent than you or I could ever be. Perhaps the idea of the church was not so novel after all; perhaps God simply did an enlargement of his original invention, the home.

If so, perhaps we husbands are best equipped to understand the intended nature and definition of the church for having struggled in everyday life with the nature and definition of our own households.

We can understand how important it is for the church to bring us, our wives, and our children into meaningful relationships with other husbands, wives, children, and single adults.

We can understand how important it is for the church to lead us by the hand and help us confess our shortcomings and failures in order to receive forgiveness and cleansing.

We can understand how important it is for the church to help us clarify our values in the midst of a relativistic world.

We can understand how important it is for the church to nudge us out of our shells into service and outreach in the name of Christ.

We can understand how important it is for the church to give evidence of the supernatural, of God at work, in the midst of a cynical society.

We can understand how important it is for the church to keep reminding us that *God can change us* for the better — that we are not locked forever in our current habits and patterns of selfish behavior.

We can understand how important it is for the church to lift our eyes from our daily problems and confront us with our Lord's love, power, justice, righteousness, and compassion.

More than once I've come home from a tough Wednesday at the office and had the refreshing experience of rejuvenating my mind and soul at the midweek service of our local church. We happen to enjoy a rather loose format on Wednesday nights, a combination of joyous singing, need-centered praying, spontaneous worshiping, fairly honest sharing by members of the audience, and practical teaching from the Word. This potpourri draws a standing-room-only crowd, and I think most of them come for the same reason Grace and I do: it's an oasis in the middle of a demanding week. One goes away feeling restored; life is put back into perspective, and we're ready to go back and face our individual challenges again.

Such an experience is evidence to us that the church of Jesus Christ is indeed a living organism. It is not just an organization. Nor is it some group called *they*. The church is *we*. *We* are the church, the living family of God, and God uses us to provide these mind-stretching, spirit-expanding times for our brothers and sisters as well as ourselves.

We are called to a rhythm of giving and receiving. Galatians 6 reminds us that we reap what we sow, in the church as well as in all of life. That concept has too long been applied only during lectures to wayward teen-agers. It has a powerful positive side as well, as the passage goes on to show. "Let us not become weary in doing good, for at the proper time we will reap a harvest if we do not give up. Therefore, as we have opportunity, let us do good to all people, especially to those who belong" — again, notice the language — "to the family of believers" (6:9,10).

So there are times when we and our wives work hard, whether teaching in the Sunday school, or singing, or playing an instrument, or going to visit someone who's ill, or doing any number of things. There are other times when we are on the receiving end of such blessings. So long as each person is giving and receiving, each is benefited, and the church fulfills its mission.

It doesn't take any special wisdom to see what happens, however, if we refuse to give. Perhaps we don't actually refuse; we just follow custom, warm the pew, keep our mouths shut, and continue being quiet, passive statistics, names on the roll and little more. Whether we do so by intention or by default, the result is the same: we are actually parasites on the life of the church! Everyone else is constantly having to pour in our direction, and we're not reciprocating. In time we become as stagnant spiritually as the Dead Sea, which has the same problem of taking in but never giving out.

There are other people in the church — and you may be one of them — who have the opposite problem. They're compulsive givers. They have to be juggling six different responsibilities at once, and they get very nervous about sitting down to receive from anyone else. It threatens their sense of importance. Unfortunately, their reserves are nearly always depleted because of their constant giving, with the result that their service is not nearly as effective or substantive as they think.

Both of these are aberrations of the intended life of

God's family. As Dr. Reuben Welch says at the end of his book *We Really Do Need Each Other:*

> You know something —
> we're all just people who need each other.
> We're all learning
>   and we've all got a long journey
>   ahead of us.
>   We've got to go together
>   and if it takes us till Jesus comes
>   we better stay together
>   we better help each other. . . .
>   Because that's how it is
>   in the body of Christ.[1]

For the past couple of years, Grace and I have seen this implemented at the grass roots by participating in a small *koinonia* group — a collection of a dozen or so people who get together every other Friday night in one of our homes to share with and support each other in our spiritual pilgrimages. We've lived through happy times together (the birth of a healthy son to one couple after an extremely troublesome pregnancy) and sad times (the sudden death of one member in a car accident) — and through it all, we've come closer to the Lord and each other.

The small group, in a way, bridges the distance between the large church and the small household; it has a foot in each. We are a subset of the church, subject to its authority; at the same time, we meet in living rooms and are never far from the joys and trials of family life. We give to each other; we receive from each other; we really do need each other.

But what if . . .

I'm aware, of course, that not everyone enjoys such a fulfilling church experience. In fact, I've often been the only person in a group of Christians who could say something positive about his church. For many, the preceding description is wishful thinking. The most common criticisms I hear are that churches are (a) dead, (b) unfriendly, (c) snobbish, (d) culturally irrelevant, (e) pessimistic, (f) theoretical instead of life-oriented, (g) a drain on the energies of their members, (h) too traditional, (i) any combination of the above.

It's true — a lot of Christians belong to churches that don't resemble families, not even a little bit. The form of worship does little to raise people's consciousness of God Almighty. They don't have meaningful relationships with other members, even though they've been in the same congregation for years. They can't point to any real spiritual change in their lives. They feel as if they're turning the wheels of a giant machine week after week with nothing to show for it.

For reasons such as these, many husbands and wives have simply dropped out of church, or have never chosen one in the first place.

The institution of the church survives without them, however, year after year, century after century. Most institutions do; they have amazing powers of self-preservation. It's incredible to stop and think about the tremendous bank of good will and don't-rock-the-boat that bolsters the institutional church in North America. The average guy in the pew does not easily bring himself to declare its faults or decry its lack of authenticity or spiritual life.

Meanwhile, the institution develops a mind of its own; it exists no longer to serve the needs of the people, but to be served *by* the people. The objection is not that members are called upon to serve, but that they are called upon to serve *a thing*, an empire, an abstraction, instead of one another. They find themselves spending major blocks of time on institutional activity rather than on building and enjoying family relationships with the Father and fellow believers.

What do we do about these things? As heads of our households, how do we promote the vitally important ministry of the church as we know it could be? How do we bring the dream alive?

Well, we do lots of things. First, we refine our understanding of the church in light of the Book of Acts and the Epistles. We make sure our dreams are biblical. Then we talk. We let our needs and desires be known. We pay our dues to the institution so that our voices can be heard and trusted. We jump in and work for change whenever the opportunity comes.

If the opportunity never comes, some may relocate, which is a difficult decision to make. All the while, however, whatever happens or doesn't happen, we keep praying — for clearer goals, for purity of motive, for the life of the Spirit to infuse us all.

This quest for the authentic church experience is important, but not so important that it can be allowed to make lousy husbands and fathers of us. There is a point at which committee sessions and prayer meetings can start to infringe upon the rest of our job description. Even more subtly, we can spend so much time *thinking* about the church (especially if we are in positions of leadership) and what we can do to improve its quality of life that there's not enough think-time left for the people closest to us.

Conversely, we cannot sink into an adversary mentality. As was said earlier, the church is *us*. For the good of both the church and our household, we must call the church to its highest and best, i.e., biblical, state "so that the lame may not be disabled, but rather healed" (Heb. 12:13). We, our wives, and our children desperately need to participate in the growth, the encouragement, the lift, and the challenge of the extended family of God. We are an intrinsic part of the household of faith. To the extent to which the church fulfills its true mission, our job is that much easier.

[1]Reuben Welch, *We Really Do Need Each Other* (Nashville: Impact, 1973).

8

What's a Christian Home?

8

What's a Christian Home?

The effectiveness of the church, of course, is not entirely ours to control. We're only individuals within the larger body. We have to work with others, our peers and spiritual leaders, to make the church beneficial in its ministry to our families.

But when we begin to think about our own households in the spiritual dimension — it's a different story. There's no one to blame but us. There are no church boards or synods standing in the way of progress. If my home reflects the nature and love of Christ on ordinary Mondays, Thursdays, and Saturdays, it's because my wife and I have determined to make it so. If the atmosphere at our house is no different from that of a non-Christian household, I can't really pass the buck to anyone else.

We husbands get this laid on us heavily from time to time, especially in Father's Day sermons. "The husband is the spiritual leader of the home," we're told. "He's the pacesetter, the priest, the representative of God for everyone in the family." (We begin slouching down into the pew at about this point.) The biblical prototypes are trotted out: Noah, who inspired his sons to work with him on a God-ordained project that seemed foolish to everyone else; Abraham, who led his family to a new country in response to divine command; Job, who sacrificed every day to atone for his children's sins; Joseph, who carefully guarded the Christ child. (We start reading the bulletin.)

Then come the bad guys, the biblical fathers who blew it: Eli, whose sons turned the tabernacle worship into an extortion-and-sex racket; Samuel, whose sons "did not walk in his ways, but . . . took bribes and perverted justice" (1 Sam. 8:3); David, who totally alienated his son Absalom and indirectly caused his untimely death; the various kings of Israel and Judah. (We check our watches.)

We know it's all true. We know our homes are supposed to be Christian homes. We don't want our kids to have to get everything spiritual from Sunday school and catechism classes. We know that the difference between a Christian family and a non-Christian family is more than just that the one goes to church on Sunday morning while the other sleeps in.

Indeed, the Puritans used to speak about the family as an *ecclesiola* — a "little church." They felt it was as important for God to be welcomed into the midst of individual families as into the larger congregation.

We all salute that. The only questions are *how* questions. How do we integrate our faith with daily living? How do we keep family prayers fresh and alive? How do we find the time? How do we avoid boredom? How much formal ritual do we need? How much spur-of-the-moment interaction?

"Back when I was a kid . . ."

If you come from a Christian heritage, you no doubt can tell impressive tales about how grandpa used to take down the old family Bible (King James Version) every evening after supper, 365 nights a year, and solemnly read a chapter to his wife and eleven children. The slightest giggle or twitch by the smallest toddler was allegedly clamped off by a severe rap on the knuckles with the heavy end of a table knife.

We won't probe the historical accuracy of all that, although it's true that many of our forefathers took family Bible reading and prayer very seriously. They set up the structures they thought necessary to communicate the Christian message in the home.

Many families continue such traditions today, with various modifications. The King James Version may be replaced by a modern paraphrase, and the father may not do all the reading, but there is still an established pattern to bring Scripture and prayer into daily life.

Even the most casual among us preserves such traditions as prayer before meals and usually before children's bedtime as well.

The questions to be asked of all such activity are: *Is it effective? Does it add up to the creating of a Christian home? Is it causing this family to "grow in the grace and knowledge of our Lord and Savior Jesus Christ"* (2 Peter 3:18)?

There are some good things to be said about the "family altar" tradition. Number one, it's regular. You don't find yourself going long stretches of time and forgetting to have spiritual input in the family.

Number two, the regularity of it says it's important. Children can't help but be impressed that this is a priority.

Number three, there's enough time over the long haul to deal in depth with a lot of spiritual concepts. Twenty minutes a day in the home is equivalent to two hours of Sunday school and church on the weekend. Over the years, it adds up.

There are possibly other advantages as well, but there are some disadvantages, too. The most obvious one is the *sameness* of what most husbands do during the family devotional time. Grandpa's children may not have moved a muscle while he read, but the chances are that at least some of the time they weren't listening either. Without variety, kids get bored, and so do adults.

Hence, we come to an important observation:

In making a Christian household, *results are more important than tradition*.

It is not so important that we continue the family practice. It is not so important that we do what we see other Christian husbands doing or advising us to do. It *is* important that we do what works.

And it's been my experience, both in my own devotional life and with Grace and the family, that *nothing works forever*. It seems that techniques and patterns last only so long, serve their purpose, and then go stale. Maybe I just have a low repetition tolerance or something, but what is neat the first week or two has a way of falling flat after a while, and I find that I need to change the structure for bringing myself and my family into meaningful communication with God.

For example: what about a simple thing like table grace? I carry on a running argument with myself over this tradition. I know the Scripture states that food is something "God created to be received with thanksgiving by those who believe and who know the truth" (1 Tim. 4:3). My problem is that the little eighteen-second prayer I often run through is not much of a carrier of thanksgiving.

Sometimes I'm really grateful that God has enabled us to have enough money to put the food on the table. At other times, I'm too hungry, or the kids are impatient, and all I want to do is get on with the eating. We utter a prayer anyway, but the effect is minimal, as evidenced by the question sometimes asked later in the meal: "Did we pray?" (You will understand why, in our particular family, we don't say, "Did we say grace?")

Once we tried shifting the prayer to *after* the meal. It was somewhat easier to put meaning into the words, "Thank you, Lord, for the food we've just enjoyed." But the tradition of decades is not easily broken, and more than once we found ourselves getting up from the table without remembering to give thanks. We eventually went back to the standard practice.

Perhaps we need to keep experimenting, finding different ways to remind ourselves that the daily food really is a gift from above and that God deserves to hear our appreciation for it. And maybe 1 Timothy 4:3 doesn't insist on prayer at every meal (heresy!), if we could be more genuinely grateful at longer intervals.

When it comes to the devotional life, Grace and I have had some exciting periods of studying the Bible and praying together. We don't do it continuously, but a couple of times each year it seems like one says to the other, "Hey, let's have devotions together for a while." At times we've gone through books of the Bible, making applications to our own lives along the way. At other times we've taken a topical approach to see what the Scripture tells us about a certain area of concern. Sometimes we've used an additional study guide or commentary; more often we've gone it alone.

When we've moved on to pray together, the synergism has been even more beneficial. Grace knows me pretty well, and I know her, so it's no use trying to be pious in front of each other. We just sort of let it all come out before the Lord. It sounds more like a three-way conversation than anything else, except that one side (the Lord's) is inaudible. Grace prays, I pray, she prays again, we wait and listen, I respond . . . sometimes we go whole paragraphs, sometimes just a sentence or two, or even a fragment, the same way a normal conversation runs. No speechmaking is allowed, or even desired.

Sometimes we kneel, sometimes we sit, and sometimes we keep our eyes open (as when praying while driving, for example!). Inevitably, we come away sensing that our heads have been cleared, that we understand a lot more about the various topics and needs we've discussed with the Lord than we did before. (We usually end up kicking ourselves for not making time to do this more often.)

I remember one particular time when our joint devotional life was crucial. The time I was in graduate school at Syracuse University was especially trying for Grace. We lived in a 2½-room efficiency apartment near the campus, and her teaching job required a 32-mile drive each day to a grade school in a small town called Elbridge. Driving is not one of Grace's favorite pastimes, so she was less than excited about commuting.

It began snowing that year on October 22, and by the time the last flakes came down on May 7, Syracuse had racked up a total of 160 inches for the winter. The terrain was hilly and the sky perpetually gray, and all in all, Grace found it depressing.

She'd come in through the drifts at the end of a school day, fix dinner, then spend the evening grading papers while I studied . . . and then, just as we were ready for sleep around eleven o'clock, the woman in the downstairs apartment would begin practicing her classical music. It wouldn't have been so bad if she'd been a good pianist, but her timing was atrocious, and Grace would spend the next couple of hours staring at the ceiling while listening to the massacre of Brahms or whoever. (Being a morning-type person, I had no trouble going on to sleep.)

There wasn't a whole lot we could do to change any of these factors. But I could sense that Grace was really having difficulty; things were piling up on her, and she was tired and worried about getting enough rest to keep functioning the next day and the next and the next.

It was then that I suggested we do a joint exploration of what the Bible has to say about peace. We knew some individual verses, of course, but for the first time we sat down with a concordance and began to pull together the whole of the scriptural message. We started a sheet of paper entitled, "Things We Want to Remember About Peace," and began making notations such as:

Phil. 4:4-7	Peace is the opposite of worry.
John 14:23-31	Peace is a real *something* that Christ deposits in us.
Gal. 5:22-25	The Holy Spirit produces peace in us.
Ps. 28:1-9	Peace is a state of mind *within* action.
2 Tim. 2:22 Rom. 14:19	Follow after, aim at peace. (The human initiative is needed, too.)

Grace clung to these verses and others for the rest of the school year. They became cords of hope to pull her through the snowy days and the discordant nights. And the change in her outlook was perceptible.

This experience is fresh in my memory because we dug out that sheet of paper a few months ago — six years later — when the person feeling harassed and in knots was not Grace but me. The combination of work responsibilities and my lack of patience with the children was getting to me, and I asked her if she'd mind a rerun of that peace study to help me get some bearings again.

Yes, it's tough to find time for this kind of interaction. It gets considerably tougher once children come into the home. You're busier, and so many of the things on your "To Do" list can't be done while the kids are awake, unless you stop parenting and just insist that they stay out of your way. You know that's not right, so you keep parenting, and wait with eagerness for the later evening hours when they're in bed so you can read and do the other things in quietness. Can you afford to give some of this precious time to a spiritual rendezvous with your wife?

Can you afford not to?

If a husband can't find the time and motivation to come with his wife into the presence of God, how is God to give guidance or input to the affairs of the household? The couple who think they can chart their own course without the help of divine direction are — in this regard — a non-Christian couple. There is no difference between their approach to marriage and that of the others on their block who admit no need of God.

Couples have to work out their own time of day and frequency. Better to get together only once or twice a week than not at all.

The serendipity times

Perhaps the best timing of all — not only for us adults but for our children as well — is the timing that happens spontaneously. While you're lying on the beach, a conversation springs up about prayer and how God answers it. Or, your son wants to know, "Who made squirrels?" Or, you're putting up Christmas decorations, and you get started talking about how to make the whole season reflect its spiritual roots.

The difference is this: you can sit everybody down and

say, "Now I'm going to tell (or read) you the story of the children of Israel crossing the Red Sea. They had just left Egypt, and the Pharaoh had changed his mind about whether to let them go, so he sent his army. . . ." Depending upon your talents as a storyteller, the response can range from medium to absolute zero.

On the other hand, let's say you're driving home from a relative's house late on New Year's Day, and your alternator goes out. You're 150 miles from home, the garages and gas stations are all closed, and it's cold and dark.

You're pretty upset, and a little worried about your limited number of options. You can drive the car on battery power only a few more miles, but you're in strange country and . . . let's face it, you don't know what to do.

If, in such a predicament, you were to say, "Well, uh . . . I don't know how we're going to get home, but I suggest we pray about it. In a way, I guess this is kind of like the jam Moses and the people were in beside the Red Sea — unless God did something, they weren't going anywhere. But the Lord showed that he could pull off a surprise, and I guess that's what we need to ask him for right now."

And suppose God does answer prayer in a dramatic way. Suppose a Good Samaritan pulls up behind you who "happens" to be the brother of the manager of an auto parts store in the next town. Within an hour, you're on your way again.

Your kids will have learned the meaning of Exodus 14 so thoroughly they'll never forget it.

Perhaps our job as Christian fathers does not depend so much on rigid traditions as it does on seizing what educators call "the teachable moment" — the time when a child is ripe for impression. I remember Nathan's fascination last summer when he was up close to a bonfire for the first time during one of our weekend trips to Wisconsin. As we sat there in the evening darkness watching the flames, I told him three fire stories from the Bible: Moses' burning bush, the three Hebrews in Babylon, and Paul on the island of Malta. The reason I know it sunk in is that he still talks about that night and the storytelling session.

God seems even to have instructed the Israelite fathers to "set up" these kinds of situations. Joshua 4:1–7 tells about the men building a huge rockpile alongside the Jordan River as they went into the Promised Land. Why? To elicit questions from their children and thus open the conversation for an account of God's power. The rockpile was intended as "a sign among you, when your children ask in time to come, 'What do those stones mean to you?' Then you shall tell them that the waters of the Jordan were cut off before the ark of the covenant of the Lord" (vv. 6,7).

A few years later, the tribes of Reuben, Gad, and Manasseh did something similar on *their* side of the river; they built "an altar of great size" (Josh. 22:10). The other tribes wanted to know why. So they explained, "We did it from fear that in time to come your children might say to our children, 'What have you to do with the Lord, the God of Israel?' . . . If this should be said . . . we should say, 'Behold the copy of the altar of the Lord, which our fathers made, not for burnt offerings, nor for sacrifice, but to be a witness between us and you ' " (vv. 24,28).

There's nothing wrong with scheduled times of Bible reading and instruction. There's nothing wrong with programs of Bible memory — at age four my parents started me memorizing verses and reviewing them from handwritten three-by-five cards, until by high-school days I'd mastered more than six hundred. But at the same time they knew how to be alert for serendipity. They could point out the hand of God in the most ordinary happenings. They were never taken off guard. It was my father who, while tucking his first grader into bed one April Tuesday night, responded clearly and simply to my question about salvation. The standard bedtime prayer had already been said, but after he'd explained the meaning of confessing my sin and placing my trust in Christ, I crawled out again and knelt beside him to ask entrance into the family of God.

I hope I have the privilege of doing the same with my own son.

A child cannot help but doubt the alleged importance of something that never gets talked about except at prescheduled times. If God is noticeable only on Sundays and for fifteen minutes after dinner each evening, then maybe he's not all the grownups claim he is.

Too often we husbands have classified the spiritual training of our children, along with mopping and dishwashing, as "women's work." Either we've been too busy or felt too inept to try to communicate the essence of the gospel to a child. Why? We don't shrink from teaching a child how to tie his shoes or change a bicycle tire or shoot free throws. The Scriptures exhort us to impart a man's touch to the spiritual area as well. Paul, in recounting his ministry in Thessalonica, writes, "We dealt with each of you as a father deals with his own children, encouraging, comforting and urging you to live lives worthy of God, who calls you into his kingdom and glory" (1 Thess. 2:11,12). It is specifically fathers who are directed to "provoke not your children to wrath: but bring them up in the nurture and admonition of the Lord" (Eph. 6:4 KJV).

Actually, the family is the perfect size for such learning and interaction. Both the public schoolteacher with a classroom of thirty and the minister with a congregation of three hundred would give a lot to be able to work with people in such small groupings as we enjoy every day in our homes.

The only valid reason I can think of for backing away from leadership in this area — and perhaps this is the real cause in many cases — is if the husband himself has no thriving relationship with the Lord. If we ourselves are not on familiar terms with God, then no wonder we hesitate to try to set the pace for our wives and/or children.

To cultivate our own rapport with God may mean getting out of bed before the rest of the family, or chopping a hole in our schedules at some point throughout the day, or making some other adjustment. The same battle for time and the same need for creative approaches that we've mentioned above apply on the individual level, too.

But as leaders who are servants, it's worth it. If God can get through to me individually, and to my wife individually, and to us as a couple, we will grow as adults, and we'll also be prepared to nurture the spiritual growth of our children. And that's what you call a Christian home.

9

Beyond Anatomy

9

Beyond Anatomy

There was an awesome day — at least as Susan Brownmiller tells it in her book *Against Our Will: Men, Women and Rape* — when the cave people first discovered that males could take sexual advantage of females, but not vice versa. In Brownmiller's feminist view, the dawning of that fact of life was as portentous as the discovery of fire or the invention of the wheel. "By anatomical fiat — the inescapable construction of their genital organs — the human male was a natural predator and the human female served as his natural prey."

And that's not all. The privilege of rape led inevitably, the author says, to a desperate female proposal for relief: a proposal called *marriage*. The prehistoric woman was glad to submit to regular rape by one man if he would, in turn, protect her from all the others. Brownmiller explains it this way:

One possibility, and one possibility alone, was available to woman. . . . Among those creatures who were her predators, some might serve as her chosen protectors. Perhaps it was thus that the risky bargain was struck. Female fear of an open season of rape, and not a natural inclination toward monogamy, motherhood or love, was probably the single causative factor in the original subjugation of woman by man, the most important key to her historic dependence, her domestication by protective mating.

. . . But the price of woman's protection *by some men* against an abuse *by others* was steep. . . . Those who did assume the historic burden of her protection — later formalized as husband, father, brother, clan — extracted more than a pound of flesh. They reduced her status to that of chattel. The historic price of woman's protection by man against man was the imposition of chastity and monogamy.[1]

So there you have it, folks — one angry woman's scenario of how the world got to be the way it is. The rest of her book is a catalog of rape across the centuries and cultures. As for the biblical account of how God instituted marriage in the Garden of Eden, as for our society's abundance of sentiments about love and sharing and commitment between husbands and wives, as for Valentine's Day and brides in white dresses holding bouquets — it's all a male chauvinist cover-up of a dastardly evil contract.

Fascinating. Also disgusting. I, for one, am not quite ready to concede that the love, warmth, devotion, and charm that emanate from my wife toward me are nothing more than payoffs for keeping the rest of the male population away from her. I would like to believe that she loves me as a complete person, that our marriage is not a case of making the best of a bad situation but rather a joint adventure toward fulfillment and joy. I believe that marriage was created by God, not by a frantic cave woman.

But having said that, I must go on to say that I can see how Susan Brownmiller came to her thesis. There's a glimmer of reality in her dismal fantasy, a glimmer that most of us would like to ignore but need to face. We must ask ourselves the question: "Do I view my marriage, in part, as a free ticket for sex?" Or, to phrase it another way, "If sex were not part of the package, would I still want to be married?"

The point is not that sex is unimportant. There's no need to disparage the fact that sexual relations with one's wife are neat experiences that feel good.

The point is that sex is a joint dimension in which both husbands and wives give pleasure to each other, thereby communicating their love in a largely nonverbal way. It is an experience in giving. It is another situation for being the servants of our wives. In fact, it may be one of the more difficult situations in which we are called upon to serve, given our Western macho traditions of sexual conquest. From boyhood on, we men have been programed in a thousand different ways to view sex as an area where we *get*, where we *take*, where we *use*. The culture is thoroughly saturated with the image of Don Juan.

But in recent years, a curious thing has happened. Women have decided to follow our example; they've realized there are some rather nice sensations for *them* to get as well. The bookstores are filled with manuals on female orgasm. The result is that many marriages are now composed of two takers, two seekers of the ultimate personal high, who may or may not happen to provide what the other person wants and needs during the process of their own quest. The traditional setup of one taker and one willing or reluctant giver is indeed a form of rape.

The newer setup of two takers is not much better, is it?

When, in contrast, we apply the model of servanthood to this area, all the dynamics change. The goal becomes the provision of her needs rather than our own. And we find, as we've noticed before, that our own needs are met along the way rather automatically. We husbands need to understand the ways and means of female orgasm. We also need to learn more about the psychological, non-physical aspects of a woman's participation in intercourse. Especially since anatomy has given us the role it has, it is all the more our responsibility to set the pattern of true sexual union, not rape.

Warm-ups and turn-ons

Granted, it can be tough sometimes to implement this lofty ideal on a practical basis. After all, what's a guy supposed to do when he slides into bed with his internal turbines already moving, and the first thing his wife says is, "Man, am I exhausted!" Surveys show that one of the most common sexual problems among couples, especially young couples, is the frequency of intercourse.

Well, there are a number of options in such a situation.

• You can argue about it. You can say, "How come? You got more sleep than I did last night."

And she'll say, "Yes, but . . . " and proceed to recount the day's various ordeals.

And you'll respond, "Gee, it'd be nice to have you save a little energy for me once in a while."

"Oh, honey, come on. . . ."

And from there on, the conversation deteriorates until you're no longer in the mood, and both of you are feeling put upon. You go to sleep reciting 1 Corinthians 7:5 to yourself ("Do not cheat each other of normal sexual intercourse" — Phillips) and wondering why your wife won't obey the Word of God!

● You can go ahead and rape her. Not by the legal definition, of course, but that's what it amounts to if you insist against her will. She may have learned over the years to keep her feelings subsurface in such situations, to "submit," to play the role pretty well, but the chances are you both know what's going on.

● You can play the martyr, with or without her knowing about it. You can say, "Well, okay — I thought we could have a little fun tonight, but if you need your sleep . . ." and you deliberately leave the sentence hanging. Such a line may manipulate her into warming up or may earn you a disgusted groan, depending upon how tired she is. You can also just roll over and say nothing and feel sorry for yourself for being married to such an iceberg. Either way, you don't go to sleep happy.

● You can start scheming a better way to turn her on next time. You begin making plans to bring home flowers tomorrow night, or be more cordial throughout the evening, or forego Monday night football, or do a few sexy things before bedtime to get her started.

Such plans are not evil in themselves; in fact, most men don't pay enough attention to the warm-up period that women seem to delight in. But the question is one of motive: are we doing such things in order to get what *we* want in the end or for the purpose of giving her pleasure and the excitement of anticipation?

This brings us to the fifth option:

● You can decide to be her servant. You can force yourself to appreciate the fact that she really is tired and that what she probably needs at the moment is not what you had in mind. You sincerely wanted to provide her with steak and lobster, but all she feels like having is a glass of milk. So that's what you give her — a gentle kiss on the forehead and a quiet "Good night."

I'm assuming in all of this that "Man, am I exhausted!" is to be taken at face value — that it's not code language for "Leave me alone, fella." If it *is* code language for some other problem of sexual adjustment, then that's another matter that needs consideration.

And as we all know, there are dozens of other adjustments to be made in a sexual relationship. We spend a lifetime working through them; frequency is just one of the pack. But many of the others — the need for gentleness on the part of the husband throughout the whole experience, the timing of releases, the place of variety, what you enjoy and don't enjoy, what she enjoys and doesn't enjoy, even ignorance about basic anatomical facts — are resolved much more easily by two people intent on serving each other than by two people out for what they can get.

Husbands and wives who are genuinely interested in pleasing their spouses have got to be willing to *talk* about sex with each other. This goes against the traditional grain — we have the assumption that if everything were going right, we wouldn't have to discuss it. We don't want to admit the existence of any problems, so we keep quiet.

How can you give your wife a greater sexual experience if you don't know how to change what you're doing? After all, you're not a mind reader. So don't pretend to be. Dr. Clifford Penner and his wife Joyce, a psychiatrist/nurse team from Pasadena who conduct seminars on sexual fulfillment, have written:

> Each of us is the best authority on what we need and like sexually. I cannot assume that I know what my partner likes. Thus it is my partner's responsibility to let me know what is pleasurable for him or her.

The Penners openly admit that everyone isn't willing to be this forthright.

> This is a slightly different approach than most of us are used to hearing from popular Christian writers. The emphasis has been much more on it being my responsibility to find out, through whatever method happens to work, what will cause my partner to respond. This approach of playing guessing games to please the other person just has not worked well when dealing with couples who are having sexual problems or wish to enhance their sexual relationship. There is a great release of tension when the couple makes and really believes the agreement that each will be responsible to let the other know what each one needs, what feels good, and what does not.[2]

Naturally, this kind of communication is a little heavy to undertake right in the middle of intercourse. It works better to discuss such things at separate times, when we're not caught up in the sweep of our emotions. The trouble is, we often don't think of it except in bed. It's like fixing a leaky roof; we keep forgetting about it until it actually rains, and at that moment it's rather awkward to try to resolve the problem.

But talk we must. We must also read. In this enlightened age, there's no excuse for being ignorant of the basic physiological facts of how our bodies work. I'm not talking about reading trashy or erotic pseudoscientific material. Every book with "M.D." after its author's name is not necessarily a sober or responsible piece of writing. I'm talking about the straightforward, nonsalacious treatments of sexual anatomy and psychology that can help us understand the way God has put us together.

There's another thing we must do, and that's get professional help if we need it. Again, the field is fraught with all manner of voyeurs and incompetents who've hung out their shingles as marriage counselors. But this cannot be allowed to prevent us from finding the bona fide specialists and listening to what they have to say.

It's interesting that such serious people as Masters and Johnson and Graber and Kline-Graber proposed a particular kind of activity that is amazingly consonant with the idea of Christian servanthood. They call it "non-demand pleasuring," in which one spouse undertakes to do whatever the other finds enjoyable, receiving no stroking or affection in return. The communication is entirely one way. The ground rule for this particular time is: no intercourse. For example, the wife lies in her husband's lap with his legs on either side, a position in which coitus is virtually impossible. He proceeds to "pleasure" her without thought of getting anything back — except the satisfaction of giving her enjoyment. He knows from earlier conversations what she likes, and he presents it to her as a gift of love.

Some of our wives would bet we'd never be able to do that; we'd have to "get ours" at some point along the way. Are they right or wrong? It may depend in part upon our willingness to obey Ephesians 5:28, where it says that "husbands ought to love their wives as their own bodies. He who loves his wife loves himself."

Periods and pregnancies

Our willingness to bend, to be flexible, and to think in terms of her needs instead of our own receives a monthly test of sorts known as The Period. For one thing, it's a test of our forbearance; for a span of up to seven days, she simply "isn't available."

That can be frustrating for us, because our sexual motors don't exactly shut down during that time. We get tired of waiting. One solution, of course, if the wife is so inclined, is to engage in a little nondemand pleasuring as described above, only in reverse. However, the initiative obviously has to be hers.

Our desires, of course, are rather minor compared to the stresses and discomfort our wives are enduring. And we keep forgetting, even though we've been told all the medical facts, how the hormone levels rise and fall to create fretfulness and depression at certain times of the month. We hear phrases like, "There's just no way for you to know what this is like" — and she's right. There isn't.

But we can learn how to make life easier for her. Whether it's fixing our own breakfast so she can sleep in, giving backrubs, or postponing our remarks about the state of the checking account, we can do a lot to accommodate the monthly period, especially in the first couple of days.

And a little wait for loving won't kill us.

There's a much greater test of our willingness to adapt and wait, of course, and that's called pregnancy. As Fitzhugh Dodson mentions in his popular book *How to Father,* the various

> physiological changes trigger drastic psychological changes in her as well. She may become moody, or irrational, or suddenly demanding. She may burst into tears over what seems to you nothing at all. Her behavior may confuse and bewilder you. It is important for you to realize that *all these things are quite normal for a pregnant woman.*
>
> In the same way that you need to make allowances for psychological changes in your wife during her monthly period, you need to make allowances for psychological changes during pregnancy.[3]

Again, there's no way for you and me to know what it's really like. Gaining twenty to thirty pounds, having to switch to a more limited, less fashionable wardrobe, being tired a lot of the time, running out of breath on a single flight of stairs, searching in vain during the later months for a comfortable sleep position, going to the bathroom fifteen times a day (and night) — it's not entirely a picnic being pregnant. Many of these limitations impinge on us as husbands; she just can't do as much as she used to, go with us all the places she'd like to. And as the months wear on, it gets frustrating for both.

At such times we need to remind ourselves whose sperm started all this. Hopefully, the decision to have a child was a joint decision, but even if it was a surprise, it didn't happen without you. You can be glad that the physical burden of carrying a fetus is not equally divided between its parents.

Eventually you find yourself facing a moratorium on sexual relations for approximately three months — the last six weeks of pregnancy and the first six weeks of recovery. Again, you don't turn into a eunuch during that time. You face the need to subjugate your desires to the greater goal of seeing this wonderful woman go through the most dramatic experience of her life — the birth of a child.

Rather than withdrawing from her, you can participate with her in this special miracle. I shall always be grateful for the Lamaze natural-childbirth training that enabled me to help Grace through her two deliveries. It took Nathan twenty-seven hours to get here, and without Lamaze, I don't know if he'd have made it or not. As I sat there in the labor room throughout the afternoon and on into the long night, timing contractions and giving the breathing instructions that would enable Grace to stay in control of the pain, I had never felt closer to her. When it all paid off at 7:20 the next morning, I was as enraptured as she. I eventually found time to write down an account of that day:

I drove home from the hospital in the bright but windy morning. It seemed like a very long time since the Volvo had last been started and I had been in the "outside world." The house was quiet when I arrived. . . . After a half-hour of telephoning, I left the house and drove toward Wheaton's Golden Bear Restaurant for pancakes.

The light turned red as I approached Gary Avenue on Jewell Road. A police car with red lights flashing stopped in the intersection to clear the way for a funeral procession. I sat watching the shiny hearse, the black limousine, the twenty or more cars of mourners, all with headlights on — and thought about birth and death, all on the same day. Little Nathan, barely three hours into life — and someone else, three days into eternity. All the rest of us stand somewhere in between those extremes. . . .

Golden Bear at 10:30 A.M. is not busy. I sat in a booth near the back, by myself. I watched the assortment of humanity before me: 195 lb. businessmen in suits, 160 lb. busboys in jeans, 125 lb. waitresses in uniforms, all so mundane. I wondered at the thought of each one of them having a special day of birth, of emerging tiny and bloody and innocent from their mothers, of sending a set of parents and a family into ecstasy. And now — how had they become so ordinary?

The pancakes finished, I went shopping for a *Chicago Tribune* (to keep) at Walgreen's, a card for Nathan at Sentiments & Sweets, three orders of flowers at Scheffler's, a car wash at Arco. Then I headed home for an unusual midday nap, setting the alarm for 1:30 P.M. in order to be back for hospital visiting an hour later.

In those hours, the inconveniences of pregnancy were a million miles from my thoughts, and Grace's as well. We were indeed "joint heirs of the grace of life" (1 Peter 3:7 RSV), and it was enchanting.

A husband comes down from such mountaintops, of course, by the time the baby comes home from the hospital to launch the reality of 2:00 A.M. feedings. The infant seems a little less cherubic than he did when three shifts of nurses were doing all the dirty work.

And in a similar sort of way, there are times throughout the course of marriage when we are less thrilled with our wives than at other times. It is an ugly but undeniable fact of life that all of us have to cope with temptation outside the marriage bond. *All* of us.

A friend of mine was once gazing out the front window of his house at a neighbor's new Corvette. "Look at that!" he exclaimed to his eight-year-old son Tommy. "Isn't that a beautiful machine? Man, wouldn't I love to have a car like that!"

Tommy, whose recent Sunday school lessons had apparently been taken from the Book of Exodus, was disturbed. "Daddy," he scolded, "you're not supposed to commit adultery!"

His confusion of the seventh and the tenth commandments is perhaps excusable. "Thou shalt not covet" can apply to women as well as sports cars. Either way, most of us don't have trouble knowing where the boundaries are; the difficulty lies in making our drives and desires conform to our moral values.

One of the most common alibis, of course, is, "I deserve to do a little messing around because my wife is such a klutz. If she'd only sharpen up, I wouldn't notice the secretaries at work so much."

You might as well face the fact that in this world there will always be younger, sharper, more shapely women than your wife. That's unavoidable. You, of course, have no way of knowing what *they* look like at 6:30 A.M., but you do know what your own wife is like at that hour, and to compare the two is unfair.

Come to think of it, there are a number of Hollywood actors who can't seem to stay satisfied with the most gorgeous 38-24-36s in the world; their infidelity and divorce problems are scandalous. It serves only to illustrate the fact that a marriage is glued together not so much by sex appeal as by the intangibles of love and commitment.

Those intangibles are intended to be permanent things that stand throughout the years, regardless of the temptations. They stand no matter where a business trip may take me; my wife may be on the other side of the continent, but her commitment to me and mine to her are right there at my side. A violation of that commitment — vicariously through film or print, or in actuality — keeps echoing in the brain for days and weeks afterward, even if it's kept totally secret.

The Scripture has some fairly heavy passages of warning that we'd do well to read periodically. First Thessalonians 4:3–6 is one of them:

> It is God's will that you should be holy; that you should avoid sexual immorality; that each of you should learn to control his own body in a way that is holy and honorable, not in passionate lust like the heathen, who do not know God; and that in this matter no one should wrong his brother or take advantage of him. The Lord will punish men for all such sins. . . .

Paul told Timothy to "flee the evil desires of youth" (2 Tim. 2:22). Don't even stand there thinking about it for a minute — run!

The really big artillery is in Proverbs 2:16–19, all of chapter 5, then 6:20 on through the end of chapter 7, and 9:13–18 — more than 75 verses in all. It seems ironic, but perhaps significant, that the world-champion polygamist should be so concerned about a clean sex life! Solomon was no prude, but even he knew that an extramarital affair is nothing but trouble.

> All at once he follows her,
> as an ox goes to the slaughter,
> or as a stag is caught fast
> till an arrow pierces its entrails;
> as a bird rushes into a snare;
> he does not know that it will cost him his life.
> (Prov. 7:22,23)

We've all known men, perhaps even close friends or colleagues, who have tragically proven the truth of those verses. We've seen careers wrecked, mental health shattered, and children devastated. And the scary part is we've known that we ourselves were vulnerable to the same downfall.

Maybe what we need to do is go ahead and admit that, by Jesus' definition, we are all adulterers. Who among us never "looks at a woman lustfully" (Matt. 5:28)? We all know good and well that our imaginations take off at times, and we do little or nothing to stop them. I'm not recommending that we pray, "Lord, forgive me for my adultery" each evening in front of our wives, but it is a sin that does need confession. Jesus was smart enough to know that we don't engage in acts we haven't first thought about. That's why he urged us to deal seriously with the thought level. It calls for unending vigilance.

If the love act is indeed an experience of giving, what can we hope to give to anyone other than our wives? We can give tension, guilt feelings, uncertainties, and apprehensions.

But to our wives we can give security, love, relaxation, affirmation, and pleasure that lasts. We can also give the experience of motherhood within an aura of joy and safety. We can lift her (and ourselves) above the passions of anatomy to the ultimate merger of two persons becoming one flesh . . . as well as one mind and spirit. These are incredible gifts, once you stop to appraise them, and they can be given by no one but husbands.

[1]Susan Brownmiller, *Against Our Will: Men, Women and Rape* (New York: Simon and Schuster, 1975), pp. 16-17.
[2]Clifford and Joyce Penner, *Sexual Fulfillment in Marriage* (Omaha: Family Concern, 1977), p. 9.
[3]Fitzhugh Dodson, *How to Father* (Los Angeles: Nash, 1974), pp. 8-9.

10
Take It Easy

10
Take It Easy

Sometimes a guy just has to relax. A man needs time to unwind, forget about responsibilities, do what feels good — golfing, fishing, hunting, reading a good book, raising sunflowers, making furniture, restoring a Model A, playing racquetball with a buddy . . . whatever.

End of chapter. What else needs to be said?

Let's not drop the subject quite yet. It's true that one individual adult with a chunk of unscheduled time can take care of himself very well. It's also true that every individual adult *needs* chunks of down-time in order to recycle, to re-create his physical and mental energies. That's one of the reasons God instituted the sabbath.

We North Americans recognize this need so well that we spend billions of dollars each year on recreation. We've managed to reduce the work week to forty hours or less to create more and more leisure time. The fastest developing region of the United States is the Sunbelt from

Florida across to California, where more and more of us are moving in order to do more relaxing outside.

But the more we take it easy, the more we realize that taking it easy is not a cure-all. Have you ever had *more* leisure time than you wanted? I've talked to men who've gone on three-week vacations, only to be climbing the walls after ten days. They realized they really didn't like to sit around and sit around and keep sitting around. They rather sheepishly ended up going back to the office ahead of schedule.

Leisure is not nirvana. Leisure is meaningful only against the backdrop of other parts of life. And for those of us who have opted to blend ourselves into a larger common life called the household, leisure is inescapably a household matter. As we are the leader/servants of so many other areas, we are the leader/servants of this one, too.

Which doesn't mean we never do things alone. We ought not to feel guilty for indulging in purely personal enjoyments at least some of the time. But since we do have wives and, in some cases, children, we need to think about balance. At the top of the next page is a chart to help you analyze how you take it easy. List ten of your common things-to-do, not necessarily in any order of preference. Just jot them down quickly as they come to mind; by the time you finish listing ten, you'll be sure to have included all the favorites.

Now go back and check off a box for each entry.

If it's a *solitary* activity — working on your car, for example, or reading a magazine — mark the S column.

If it's something you do with one or more members of your *family* — playing softball with your kids or going out to dinner with your wife — use the F column.

If it's something you do with *outside* people — such as Monday night basketball in the YMCA league or playing

150

HOW I TAKE IT EASY

		S	F	O
1.	_____	☐	☐	☐
2.	_____	☐	☐	☐
3.	_____	☐	☐	☐
4.	_____	☐	☐	☐
5.	_____	☐	☐	☐
6.	_____	☐	☐	☐
7.	_____	☐	☐	☐
8.	_____	☐	☐	☐
9.	_____	☐	☐	☐
10.	_____	☐	☐	☐

your tuba in the community orchestra — mark the box in the O column.

How does it look? With whom are you doing most of your relaxing? If you don't have many checks in the middle column, what does that tell you?

In many marriages, there is indeed a great wall between husbanding/fathering and leisure. Both spouses have an understanding that the husband is entitled to a certain amount of "off-duty" time, as if with a switch he could turn off his regular identity and turn into a man-about-town. Sometimes this is formally scheduled as a weekly "night out with the boys."

Let me repeat: there's nothing particularly evil about a man relaxing by himself or with nonfamily individuals. But it *is* a problem if he so divides his life into two parts that the one is considered fun and the other drudgery. This is neither helpful nor fair. True husbanding is not a drag. A man can have some of the most pleasurable and rewarding times of his life with his family. A lot depends on his own perspective.

TV and other pursuits of pleasure

You're a rare breed if you didn't list TV as one of your ten relaxation activities. But how did you classify it — solitary or family?

The social critics of our time have rather convincingly pointed out that TV watching is rarely a shared experience. The fact that other family members may be in the same room, even sitting on the same couch with you and digging into the same sack of potato chips, doesn't alter the fact that the communication is pretty unidirectional. The tube is the sender of messages to you, a receiver, and also to your wife and/or child, other receivers — but that's the end. You don't interact with each other beyond a common laugh or groan once in a while. You don't even have a medium for giving feedback to the people on the screen (which may partially explain the quality of programing these days).

And if the messages being emitted happen to be messages about the progress of the Oakland Raiders against the defensive unit of the Pittsburgh Steelers, chances are your wife isn't even in the room to share your groans. Only when we go to the bother of looking for a program of interest to both and following it up with some dialogue can TV watching be called a shared form of leisure activity.

This problem is most inflamed on New Year's Day, when football games run nonstop for around eleven hours of what is commonly assumed to be a family holiday. Many husbands and wives are never so near and yet so far from each other as on January 1. I'm not saying that football should be *verboten* on holidays; I'm simply saying that all of us need to be aware year-round of TV's great power to isolate us right under our own roofs.

My current battle happens to be with the six o'clock news. If I had my way, I'd choose to come home from work, sit down to eat with Grace and the kids, then take my dessert into the family room for a half-hour of watching Chancellor and Brinkley. It's a relaxing thing for me to do, and it's also a free source of up-to-the-minute information.

The only trouble is, it doesn't mesh with what has come to be known at our house as the Grizzly Hour — that period from about four-thirty in the afternoon on through to bedtime when young children are tiredest and crankiest. Parents need to be at their best during the Grizzly Hour, inventing creative things to do and heading off potential conflicts. Grace has already spent a good deal of her creativity throughout the day and is looking forward to the charms of a fresh, new voice. When all that new voice can come up with is, "Nathan, go play in your room — I'm watching the news," the scene has a way of deteriorating.

There *are* ways for me to relax with Nathan and Rhonda and Tricia instead of apart from them. And there are ways for me to get the news during less critical times of the day, too. It all comes down to whether I'm willing to be a servant or not.

One of the tougher skills we husbands have to acquire is the ability to genuinely enjoy playing with young children. Playing is not a waste of time; it's the primary learning activity for kids, and if their dads are willing to participate enthusiastically, an invaluable bond is formed between parent and child.

I remember in the early months of fathering how frustrated I got trying to spend time with my son and accomplish some adult task at the same time. My conscience told me I needed to sit on the floor and stack blocks with Nathan, that I shouldn't wait until he could hit a baseball to start playing with him. But what inefficiency! Surely I could redeem the time by reading a news magazine *while* I stacked blocks.

Wrong. Nathan could tell I wasn't really interested, and I could tell I wasn't comprehending a third of what I was trying to read. It took a while to convince myself that spending time with a child, even an infant or a toddler, is *worthwhile in itself,* an activity worthy of my full attention. Better to spend twenty minutes playing — and enjoying it — followed by twenty minutes of reading, than to attempt forty minutes of trying both and doing neither well.

Heaven help the preschooler whose father thinks puzzles and dot-to-dot books are dumb. Heaven help the grade schooler whose dad can't be bothered with bugs and Barbie dolls. The same man will be hard-pressed to build any kind of relationship once his kids reach the teen-age years. As Maureen Green says in her book *Fathering,* "The biggest deprivation children suffer is not having been enjoyed by both parents."[1]

And the beautiful thing is that if our values are in the right places, our time spent with children doesn't have to be a chore. It can be genuine fun, which makes it good for us as well as for them. Mrs. Ethylene Nowicki, mother of the famous ice skater Janet Lynn, told me once during an interview while I was ghostwriting her daughter's book, "My husband and I made a decision early in our marriage: we decided that for the first twenty years or so we'd do things *with* our kids. We said there would be enough time later on for us, but while the kids were growing up, we'd invest the time in their lives."

By the looks of the awards and trophies that festoon the Nowicki home — not only Janet's but the other three children's as well — it's obvious that their decision was a brilliant one. Little did this parent realize that "doing things with the kids" would take her from Rockford, Illinois, to points as diverse as Davos, Switzerland, and

Sapporo, Japan, en route to her daughter becoming an Olympic bronze medalist.

Games we play

There's a lot to be said for sports and games as a way for couples and families to have fun together. It can be as vigorous as football on the lawn or as quiet as a father-son chess match; the options are more numerous than you'll ever have time for. Games make it easy for us to get in touch with each other, to interact, even to stretch each other's abilities. My family happens to be fanatical about word games, everything from Probe to Scrabble to a corny but funny thing called the Dictionary Game. Other families generate more of their togetherness with athletics. Both are effective in helping parents and children as well as husbands and wives to relate and recreate together.

But something else needs to be said about games: they're a little dangerous. They have the potential of harming the household and ripping up relationships if competition gets out of hand. Competition is a powerful motivator so long as it's in harness, but left to run wild, it can devastate. If we join in the combat of a game to give the other person a challenge to try and overcome, we have done him a service. But if we join in combat for the thrill of humiliating the other person, of proving how much better we are, of grinding him into the dirt, we've degraded both him and ourselves.

A lot of gung-ho husbands and fathers don't understand that distinction. (Neither, for that matter, do a lot of coaches and managers.) I was fortunate enough to have a father who once forbade me and my foster brother to keep score after the Ping-Pong rivalry between us had gotten raw. He said, "For the next couple of weeks, you guys can practice all you want — but no scorekeeping. You both need to cool down." It worked.

Competition may be even tougher to handle between husbands and wives. Everything's fine, of course, so long as we keep winning, and some of our wives have been programed by social custom to make sure that happens. But more and more women are rejecting such nonsense. We do, too — in theory. Yet when we actually lose a game, especially one that requires brawn as well as brains, some of us can't take it.

You can tell a lot about a marriage by watching and listening to its partners play a game together. All kinds of repressed hostilities can come to the surface. The opportunities for vengeance, for embarrassment, and for reprisal are just waiting to be seized by a mate with an ax to grind or a grievance to air. The husband and wife don't necessarily have to be opponents in the game. In fact, it is often even more revealing when they have to cooperate with each other as members of the same team.

In a cover story entitled "Sex & Tennis: The New Battleground," *Time* magazine outlined the pitfalls of mixed doubles:

> If there is one serpent most easily discernible in the Garden of Eden togetherness that Americans hope for from tennis, it is the American husband. . . . He is found guilty of coaching and poaching — *i.e.*, taking shots from his wife's side of the court. Of preaching and reaching and teaching. Of cheating and bleating. Of serving too fast. Of serving too slow. Of hitting the ball right at his female opponent. Of not hitting the ball right at his female opponent. Of bad tennis, bad sportsmanship and, above all, a bad mouth. . . . "Run! Run!" "Hit the ball. *Hit* the ball." "Up! Up!" and, maddeningly above all for women partners, "Outta the way! I got it! I got it!"[2]

The same article reprinted a cartoon from Bil Keane's *Deuce and Don'ts of Tennis* showing a husband and wife in bed, facing opposite directions, both as far to the outside edge as possible. The husband is saying, "Cripes! You don't think I double-faulted on the final point of the tie breaker *on purpose*, do you?"

Games can be a delightful unifying factor in a household; they can also be a wedge that divides and destroys. The choice is ours.

The hassle-free vacation

One particular time of year, of course, is given almost entirely to recreation and leisure: the vacation. At no other time do we have so many free hours in a row to take it easy.

Yet vacations can be mixed blessings. Psychologists tell us that husbands and wives are more likely to argue on vacation than at almost any other time. It's not hard to see why. The most frequent disputes are about:

• *Money*. The splurge mentality takes over . . . forget the budget . . . we've been saving all year for this . . . we're going to have a good time or else! There is, of course, a limit to the amount that can be spent, and not everyone's wishes can always be accommodated. So some hard decisions have to be made, and no one wants to lose.

The financial squeeze is undoubtedly the cause of the rise of camping in recent years. What's neat about camping is that it allows you to relax and do a lot of different things together as a family without spending money every time you turn around. Granted, the equipment costs something, but once you own it, that's it, and the nightly fees aren't much. In some cases, even the equipment can be borrowed or rented. Meanwhile, camping offers dozens of built-in opportunities for husbands to get reacquainted with their wives and kids — everything from gathering firewood to riding bikes to staying dry during rainstorms. Even the housekeeping tasks of dishwashing and bedmaking can be profitably shared.

● *Discipline of children.* The other fifty weeks of the year, we're not home during the day to observe how our wives handle things. Suddenly the reality of round-the-clock child care hits us. We discover that our reserves of patience are not as great as we thought.

And the demand for patience is greater when you have kids cooped up in a car all day than when you're at home. On a long trip, the car can become a pressure cooker of tension if the husband isn't sensitive to the need for —

1. Frequent stops. Some of us cherish our reputations, established during college days, for marathon driving — Nashville-to-Los Angeles in twenty-seven hours straight through, and all that. We've always prided ourselves on our ability to get to a place faster than anyone else. But with kids who need to stretch and run off excess energy every hour and a half — forget it. To keep pushing only puts the entire family on edge.

2. Games and activities while driving. Grace and I have some friends who each year before vacation assign their five children to collect their own "fun-paks" of things to do in the car. Parents are wise to bring along some extras themselves.

3. Simple conversation. Why do so many of us seem to clam up once we're behind the wheel? Driving time is great time for talking about ordinary things, special things, spiritual things, anything. It beats watching the mileposts in silence.

● *Choice of activities/location.* If your idea of a vacation is a fishing/canoeing trip in northern Ontario, while hers is a Sheraton hotel next to three shopping centers, and the kids are thinking of Disneyland . . . you've got some work to do before you pull out of the driveway. The task is to reconcile the desires of each and somehow create an experience that will be fun for everyone. What you *don't* want to do is promise features that probably aren't going to happen once you start.

You may have to do one person's favorite one year and someone else's the next. Or you may split up, letting a teen-ager go to a camp or to a friend's or relative's house while you and your wife head a different direction. If your children are very young, the difference between Six Flags Over Texas and the local amusement park is minimal — and if it would take three days to drive to Six Flags, you're far better off hitting the local spot on a Saturday and planning a strictly adult vacation for yourself and your wife. If you don't want to be away from the children that long, why not a series of weekends at a nearby hotel or resort?

But having said that, let's be careful not to forfeit the togetherness that a family vacation can engender. Some parents are all too happy to dump their kids summer after summer. There are many things we can do together, and the benefits are significant.

Vacations are probably more strategic for our wives than for either the kids or ourselves. Why? Because wives carry the major responsibility for the work of the household . . . seven days a week. We enjoy a day or two of "vacation" at the end of each week during which we temporarily forget about our jobs. Not so the housewife. Thus, in terms of pure recycling and change of scenery, she is the neediest.

As a matter of fact, vacations are but part of the relief she needs. Weekend dinners and excursions are even more refreshing for her than for us. They don't have to be expensive. Grace and I once spent a delightful day on my birthday taking in free things of Chicago — the Museum of Science and Industry, a photography exhibit in the lobby of a downtown bank, the Chicago Board of Trade, a historical museum, State Street window-shopping. You might want to sit down with your wife sometime and make a list of all the things the two of you could do for less than five dollars. Keep adding to the list as things come to your mind, as you read the Sunday paper, and as friends happen to mention places they've gone and evenings they've enjoyed.

In the final analysis, taking it easy is not as dependent upon externals — money, travel, sports equipment, electronic gadgetry — as it is on our internal capacity to find enjoyment not only in Hawaiian scuba diving but in rainy Saturdays at home as well. If we can give leisure its proper place in our lives and strike the right balance with the other more serious ingredients, we'll not only live longer ourselves, but we'll have a happier, more relaxed, more integrated household along the way.

[1]Maureen Green, *Fathering* (New York: McGraw-Hill, 1976), p. 180.
[2]"Sex & Tennis," *Time*, Vol. 108, No. 10 (Sept. 6, 1976), p. 42.

11

Sickness
(What a Pain)

11

Sickness
(What a Pain)

What causes stress?

Not long ago a couple of doctors at the University of Washington Medical School set out to answer that question. They studied the most common causes, the things that upset us, and tried to rank them on a numerical scale.

What they came up with was the Holmes-Rahe Stress Test, a list of forty-two events that range from the death of a spouse (100 points) to a minor violation of the law (11 points). By going down the list and checking off what's happened to you in the past year, you can get an idea of how much stress has been accumulating inside you, whether you're aware of it or not.

It is significant that, based on their research, the two professors ranked personal injury or illness near the top of the list — 53 points. The only things more upsetting than getting hurt or getting sick were marital separation or divorce, a jail term, and the death of a close family member. It's *less* of a jolt to get married (50 points), to get fired from your job (47 points), to be reconciled to an estranged spouse, or to retire (45 points each).

And very next in the hierarchy of stress-causing events comes change in a family member's health (44 points).

. . . We already knew all that, didn't we? We hate being sick ourselves, and we hate what happens to the household when anyone in it is sick. We hate the bills that sickness brings. We hate everything about it.

We hate it enough that we go to considerable effort to prevent it — everything from taking vitamins, to insisting that our kids wear coats when they don't want to, to installing humidifiers to cut down on wintertime sore throats, to about anything else we can think of. Still, it's not enough. We continue to get sick. Not as often as people did in the past, or as often as we would if we didn't take precautions, but it still happens. And it's hard on us.

Why it's tough

When somebody at your house comes down with the flu, or when a more serious illness invades, some rather deep-running things happen to the equilibrium of the household. Often we don't recognize them; we're too busy feeling awful (if we're the person who's sick), or worrying (if it's our wives or children), or trying to keep the household going — getting meals on the table, etc. We don't stop to observe the scene as a whole.

But what's going on is that one member of the family is no longer able to make his or her normal contribution to the life of the household. If the household is composed of only two persons, that means a loss of 50 percent! Even if you have several children, it still means you're missing a major chunk of the life and energy that in normal times make up your family.

The rest have to pick up the slack. If your wife's in bed,

someone else — probably you — has to cook. If you're in bed, someone else has to make sure the car has gas. If your son's sick, someone else has to do his paper route. All this switching around causes pressures that we don't normally face. It creates a special test of our willingness to "serve one another in love" (Gal. 5:13).

And as if that weren't enough — the overall work load of the household is increased above its normal level by the need to take care of the sick person himself. He may need peace and quiet so he can sleep, even when it's daytime and the kids are accustomed to playing their kazoos. He may need special kinds of food. He may need help eating the food. He may need help with certain kinds of therapy or exercise. He probably needs medication or, in some cases, even injections.

In other words, there is more than the average amount of work to be done, and there's one less person in the household to do it. No wonder we get uptight.

Many of us men have particular difficulty coping with sickness because, of all the family members, we're the most efficiency-minded. Our jobs have done it to us. We think in terms of accomplishing certain blocks of work within certain time-frames; we're constantly thinking about ways to get more done faster. Efficiency is a key word in our vocabulary.

In contrast, our kids enjoy the prerogatives of childhood, one of which is to fritter away hours upon hours as they wish. Even our wives, at least most of them, are not as clock-conscious as we are. As the old saying goes, "A mother's work is never done" — and since that is true, mothers usually take a somewhat less intense attitude toward their work. There's always tomorrow.

Thus, it's not hard to see that sickness is more disrupting to our life style than to any other member of the family. If we get sick, it means staying home in the daytime — and that's a major shock all by itself. We've never seen what happens around the house at ten-thirty and noon and three o'clock. We don't know how to act. At least when our wives or children get sick, they remain on familiar turf. We're out of our element, and we can't help but wonder what's going on at the office or the plant or the construction site, where we'd prefer to be at this hour.

Factors such as these lead women to say that men don't cope well with sickness, are "big babies," etc. They're often correct. Part of it definitely has to do with our efficiency mindset. But another part has to do with the traditional masculine self-image of toughness and independence. Many of us can't stand to be weak or vulnerable. So when sickness does precisely that to us, we turn cranky. We know we don't look like big, strong he-men any more, and that makes us mad. Our ego has been bruised.

Remember the story of Nebuchadnezzar in the Old Testament? There was a point at which God sent him into severe mental and physical trauma "until you have learned that the Most High rules the kingdom of men and gives it to whom he will" (Dan. 4:32). Is it not possible that God sometimes does the same to us in order to cut us down to size?

"I'm all right, Jack" vs. "Must be cancer"

The more we face illnesses — both our own and those of our household — the more we come to realize the importance of the mental or attitudinal battle that accompanies the physical. The doctor does his thing against the germs and viruses; concurrently, we must do ours against the despondency and discouragement that is an intrinsic part of being sick.

After all, there's a limit to what we can do on the physical front. But there's a great deal we can do to control our minds. The story is told of Bill Klem, famous National League umpire who sometimes used to wait a bit before announcing his decision after a pitch.

One day a young, impetuous rookie was on the mound, and Klem's delays started to irritate him. After unloading one pitch, he hollered in, "Come on, Bill — what is it?"

Klem took off his face mask and glared back. Then he drawled, "Son — it ain't nothin' till I call it somethin'."

We husbands have a choice as to what the curve balls of illness are to be called in our homes. Most of our wives take the cue from us. And from that point, the two of us can set the atmosphere for the rest of the household. We can call a situation a major tragedy, or a moderate difficulty that is quite surmountable. We can call it a big fake on the part of the person in bed, or we can pronounce it legitimate. We can call it a torpedo to the family budget, or we can call it another one of those unexpected challenges that we'll get through somehow. We can call it a sadistic slap from a capricious God, or we can admit that we human beings don't always understand the reasons why — and don't have to. In the realm of attitudes, sickness ain't nothin' till we call it somethin'.

As with Bill Klem's balls and strikes, of course, the call has to bear some resemblance to reality. We cannot pretend that a doctor's diagnosis of leukemia is trivial. But neither should we act like appendicitis is the end of the world. My wife and I have a good deal of adjusting to do in this area, since I tend to underplay sickness and she tends to overplay it. When I was growing up, we seldom went to the doctor; the assumption was that the less spotlight given to illness, the less it would be around. In her family, health discussions seemed to get more air time.

So we've had more than one disagreement about what to call various sets of symptoms. We haven't completely resolved the problem yet, but we're working on it. On two or three different occasions I've brushed off a baby's crying in the night as simply teething or bad dreams; finally, Grace has persuaded me that it ought to be checked by the pediatrician, and it has turned out to be an ear infection that definitely needed medication.

On the other hand: as I write this chapter, two-year-old Rhonda is wearing a cast, having broken her right arm while playing last Thursday. The doctor warned us to keep watching the fingers until the swelling recedes to make sure the cast isn't cutting off circulation, especially during sleep. Grace spent most of the weekend stewing over whether Rhonda's right fingers were exactly as warm and as pink as her left ones, while I saw almost no difference. As of yesterday and today, the swelling is gone and the danger is past.

It's hard at such times for a lot of us men not to turn sarcastic ("Good grief — what a hypochondriac!") or to accuse the other person of malingering. Such biting remarks may feel good as we unleash them, but they don't do much for the atmosphere of the household in general. Instead, we must find ways to be constructive; we must ask ourselves, "What can I do and say that will help my wife (or child) get over this as soon as possible?"

So many of us feel awkward in the face of sickness. Especially when our children are ill, we automatically think, *Well, my wife will take care of it. She's good at that.* Not any better than we can be. Serious research into the differences between males and females has found that "the two sexes appear to be equally 'empathic,' in the sense of understanding the emotional reactions of others."[1] We can respond in a loving way to pain, to nausea, and to fever as well as our wives can — if we will.

But along with our empathy, we must also look toward recovery. There has to be a balance between "You poor darling" and "It's not so bad." It is a great ministry to let the sick person know he's not alone, that we care deeply and hurt deeply along with him. It is also a ministry to establish a climate of hope, an expectancy of getting well, in the midst of a sickroom.

And the neat thing is that God has so many different ways of bringing about healing. He's built into our bodies an amazing recuperative power, from white corpuscles in the blood that kill off harmful bacteria to the ability to grow new skin and tissue wherever needed. He's given all kinds of natural and synthetic substances for the medical profession to use. He's also reserved for himself the right to intervene directly and correct problems that baffle laymen and doctors alike. He is a God of many options. And since he's a loving Father who — all other things being equal — prefers not to see his children suffer, he uses his options continuously.

It is only natural, then, that we as earthly husbands and fathers present our needs to him and ask for his healing. A lot of the flap over divine healing in this century has arisen over methodology — *how* God restores our health. I grew up in a culture that considered it righteous to call for divine intervention and a lapse of faith to solicit a doctor's help. Other Christians have erred in the opposite direction; they've said that in our modern, enlightened era, God heals through doctors only, and any prayer for healing is quackery. Well, God is not to be put into a box. He can — and does — restore the human body however he pleases. Scriptures such as James 5:14–18 most clearly exhort us to pray when we're sick and to ask others to pray for us. Nowhere in Scripture, however, are we told that this is the only method, or that medical help is a believer's cop-out.

Practically speaking, the prayer of faith is a major factor in controlling the atmosphere of our homes when sickness strikes. It is a symbol of hope. It is a positive voice in the midst of negativsm. Through it, we remind ourselves that all is not lost, that the supernatural is entirely possible, and that God our Father is still in control.

As a husband, I sometimes find myself waiting far too long before I pray about some of the minor illnesses that come along. I keep thinking that they'll go away by themselves, and sometimes it's several days before I wake up and say, "Hmmm, the Bible told us to pray about things like this." We've had some rather quick recoveries (I prefer to believe they were direct healings) at our house once I took hold of my responsibility as the leader/servant of the household and had a definite time of prayer. Grace and I have then asked each other, "What took us so long?"

I'm not saying that God will heal every time we ask him. In fact, the evidence shows that he doesn't. We have to face the fact that sometimes a family member doesn't naturally recuperate, and medicine is unable to help, and God doesn't intervene supernaturally — and the person dies. Such an event has to be the worst shock a household experiences. Drs. Holmes and Rahe put the death of a spouse at the top of their stress list, and they didn't even try to rank the death of a child. It would probably have been 300 stress units or more. Whole books have been written on the subject, and all of us need to become more realistic about these possibilities. It's not good to be morbid, but neither is it wise to assume that we and the members of our household are immortal.

Nevertheless, until death becomes unavoidable, we must remain on the side of life and health. We must refuse to live in fear. We must do all that we can to be healthy, and ask God to do the rest. John Donne, the famous English poet and clergyman, was stricken with a devastating illness that kept him down throughout the winter of 1623. In spite of his suffering, he managed to record his thoughts during that time, which were published the next year as *Devotions upon Emergent Occasions*. One passage summarizes well his hope and ours in the face of sickness:

> Pray in thy bed at midnight, and God will not say, "I will hear thee tomorrow upon thy knees at thy bedside"; pray upon thy knees there then, and God will not say, "I will hear thee on Sunday at church." God is no tardy God, no presumptuous God; prayer is never unseasonable; God is never asleep, nor absent.[2]

[1]Eleanor E. Jaccoby, *The Psychology of Sex Differences* (Stanford, Calif.: Stanford University Press, 1974), p. 351.
[2]John J. Pollock, comp., *We Lie Down in Hope: Selections from John Donne's Meditations on Sickness* (Elgin, Ill.: David C. Cook, 1977).

12

The Rest
of the Clan

12

The Rest of the Clan

If a pollster came to your front door with the following questions, how would you answer? Take a pencil and mark your responses.

1. Please think for a moment about the way things operate at your house compared to that of your parents. Would you say the two are —
   - ☐ very similar?
   - ☐ generally similar?
   - ☐ only partly similar?
   - ☐ generally different?
   - ☐ very different?

2. Now please think for a moment about the way things operate at your house compared to that of your parents-in-law. Would you say the two are —
   - ☐ very similar?
   - ☐ generally similar?
   - ☐ only partly similar?
   - ☐ generally different?
   - ☐ very different?

Very similar? You're probably among a minority. The continuous changing and shifting that's going on in twentieth-century society means a lot of people conduct their households differently from their parents. The extent of those differences — and how the younger and older generations choose to view them — are often the determining factor between compatibility and open warfare.

All through this book we've been developing a concept, a set of values and definitions, of what a household is. We've talked about a particular perspective on communication, money, spiritual life, and a number of other things.

But we don't happen to live in airtight bubbles where we can work out our life styles by ourselves. Our parents and parents-in-law have been thinking about how we ought to live, too. In fact, they've had the jump on us — they've been thinking, planning, dreaming, wishing, and churning all this over for twenty years or more before we even started! Long ago, while we were engrossed with bubble gum cards and Little League, their minds were at work: *Someday, when they get married and set up a home, it'll be like this. . . .*

And now, we've done it.

And in at least some ways, it's not at all what they were expecting.

That's a tough break for any fifty-year-old. Our parents were counting on us to think so highly of their values and the example they set that we would go out and produce a carbon copy. And we didn't do it. *Why not? Don't they appreciate all that we tried to instill? Why aren't they using their heads? Are they going to have to learn everything the hard way?*

Such traumas can affect everything from the flow of conversation to the condition of their blood pressure. In a way, their side is understandable. At their age, they don't deserve any more hassles or worries. We love our parents and want to please them.

But on the other hand, we cannot afford to perpetuate their marital mistakes and weaknesses for the sake of family unity. We have a vision of the caring, serving, loving, Christian household, and the crucial questions are:

1. Does the rest of the clan (parents, parents-in-law, siblings on both sides) comprehend our vision? Do they understand what we have in mind? Do they grasp the dynamics at work?

2. If they do comprehend "where we're at," does this mesh with their long-cherished expectations?

If their definitions are our definitions, a beautiful synchronization is the result. The disagreements of childhood, especially adolescence, are past; we and our parents can finally get in step with one another on a permanent basis. We see so much of the logic they wanted us to see in earlier years. At the same time, they see the reward of two decades of work and sacrifice as we take our place in adult life and become productive. The need for authoritative direction is gone; we can be friends, equals, comrades.

Our children cannot help but sense the solidity of this relationship. A great continuity is formed as they find themselves surrounded not only by parents but grandparents and uncles and aunts, all of whom share the same set of family values and priorities. The child gradually realizes that he is part of a lasting, ongoing, tried and tested unit.

If, however, the rest of the clan does not define the household as we do, there *will* be conflicts. It's unavoidable. Any time two groups of people with differing philosophies make contact with each other in an area of vital interest to both, an extra measure of Christian grace and flexibility is needed.

Some of the common difficulties are:

● *Allocations of time.* You and I are busy people. In chapters 5, 6, and 10, we discussed how to dispense the time available among all the things we need to do. We've got a lot going.

Maybe your parents don't agree with your allotments. They think you ought to be carving out more time for them. Maybe her parents think you're too job-oriented, and their sweet little darling is virtually a widow.

Stop and think a minute. They're most likely in one of two stages of adult life: (1) the "empty nest" stage (approximately 50-65), when you and your brothers and sisters have left home and their responsibilities are suddenly much lighter, or (2) outright retirement. In either case, they're slowing down, taking life easier, and trying to cope with more leisure hours than they've had since their own school days. Meanwhile, you're charging around as busy as you've ever been. Your pace may leave them breathless — as well as envious of the fact that your productivity is still high while theirs is tapering.

It's not unusual, is it, that they should express themselves about your use of time?

● *Allocations of money.* While you and your wife are still in the process of fine-tuning your approach to fiscal management, your parents are heading into an adjustment that can be just as rugged: how to keep from starving in old age. Their earning power only has a few more years to go, or else it has already dropped to zero — no wonder they're suddenly very aware of financial reserves. Meanwhile, you're buying houses, cars, and clothes like there was no tomorrow — sometimes wisely, sometimes foolishly.

They remember hard times, especially the 1930s

(when today's retirees were starting married life), and they would do anything to spare you a similar ordeal. Unfortunately, their good intentions can sometimes degenerate into meddling.

The situation can get even stickier if you and your wife borrow some of their money. Now they occupy the role of creditor as well as parent. And you are a debtor as well as a son. It takes a great deal of discipline to keep the two separate. If, on a strictly business basis, it makes good sense for them to invest in your project, and they can refrain from using the debt, however subtly, as a psychological lever in other areas, a parent-child loan can be all right. Otherwise, see your local banker.

• *Number of children.* I've never been a grandparent, so I'm sure I can't fully describe the emotional thrill it brings. But it's understandable that older people would get rather excited about their children starting or enlarging the family. The third generation is, to them, a symbol of hope, new life, almost a reincarnation; their name is preserved and extended; the dynasty lives on.

So if you and your wife seem not to be cooperating in this noble cause — if, for example, you're preoccupied for several years with finishing an education or accumulating a down payment *in order* to create a more stable household in which to raise children — you'll just have to endure the various little hints and suggestions. You've got to march to the beat of your own drummer.

• *Discipline of children.* Grandparents can run a wide gamut. On the one end are those who see it as their gleeful privilege to spoil your kids rotten. On the other end are those who are sure your kids are going to the dogs, and they've been given back-up responsibility to straighten them out since you won't.

Hopefully, your parents and your wife's are somewhere in between. Grandparents can make a tremendously positive contribution if they remember that these are *your* kids and are willing to follow and reinforce your leads.

- *Politics*. It's highly possible — even probable — that you and your parents and in-laws don't see eye-to-eye on public affairs. You probably never will. It becomes even tougher when someone mounts a soapbox and tries to convert the rest of the family to his side. Some families are skilled at discussing political issues at the conceptual level and can learn a great deal from one another in the process. Others, however, can't seem to keep the discussion from turning into a verbal brawl.

- *Reunions and holidays*. It took me a while to realize why I'm occasionally frustrated at a family gathering. We'll drive 300 miles to be together, and then it sometimes seems like we're not having a good time. Why? It's no one's fault in particular; the problem arises from the fact that family get-togethers take a good deal of logistical planning, not only for meals and sleeping accommodations, but in terms of how to fill the time. We've got a day or a whole weekend together — what shall we do besides sit around and talk?

The restlessness results because this particular situation has *no designated leader*. My dad long ago stopped telling us what to do, now that we're grown. But it seems presumptuous for any of the rest of us to take charge — especially me, being the youngest of the siblings. (Birth order is a very real factor even in adulthood.) What time shall we eat? What games shall we play? Who shall pay for what?

The answers to these questions have to be reached by *consensus,* which is always tricky for people who aren't with one another on a day-to-day basis. I'll say something like, "Well, uh, maybe we could do such-and-such," and then timidly wait to see if anyone endorses my idea. It can be a clumsy, time-consuming process!

Full-scale family reunions that involve large numbers cannot help but throw together people who hardly know one another. It's almost like getting together all the left-handed people on your block; they don't really have that much in common. It takes more than a common surname to make the day enjoyable.

One part of our clan heritage that most of us want to preserve, however, are our holiday traditions, especially Christmas. All newlyweds face the task of merging their two sets of ritual. Grace comes from a gifts-on-Christmas-Eve family while I come from a gifts-on-Christmas-morning family. She was accustomed to placing gifts under the tree, while my parents had made a point of drawing our young eyes to the Nativity crèche by placing gifts there. Such relatively "minor" things are laden with great emotional and sentimental freight built up over twenty or more Christmases. They can be the makings of real conflicts.

The obvious solution is to blend the best of both and create a new, original family tradition. This past year Grace and I chanced onto an innovation that we're both eager to try again. Her parents were with us for the traditional Scandinavian Christmas Eve dinner, and as we opened their gifts afterward, the kids were very wound up and the whole scene seemed more like bedlam than anything else. What blew my fuse was when Nathan, having torn through several nice presents in less than fifteen minutes, looked up and whined, "Is that all I get?"

I reprimanded him, apologized to his grandparents, and made a silent resolution that Gift Time No. 2, scheduled for the next morning, would be different. Late that night, after everything had calmed down and the wrappings and ribbons had been squashed into the trash can, I went to the basement and got six cardboard boxes. I sorted out the remaining gifts as follows:

- Gifts *from* Nathan
- Gifts *from* Rhonda
- Gifts *from* Tricia
- Gifts *from* Mom and Dad
- Gifts *from* Grandma and Grandpa Merrill
- Gifts *from* our friends.

The next morning when everyone got up, the boxes with signs attached were sitting on a high table. I explained that each of us would take turns getting a gift from his box and *giving* it to someone else in the room, and that we'd all watch to see what had been given before going on to the next gift. By shifting the spotlight from getting to giving, I hoped to restore some of the meaning we'd lost.

It worked. Even the twins at twenty-one months of age seemed to catch the idea as they toddled around placing gifts in other people's hands. Since my parents weren't with us, the children were allowed to make their presentations too. The whole experience was quieter, not at all frenzied, and reflected the symbolism of God giving us his Son. When, later in the day, I asked Nathan, "What did you *give* for Christmas?" he was able to list a number of things, and the pride that showed on his face told me he was pleased.

Christmases as well as birthdays are times when *my* traditions and *her* traditions need to be merged and redeveloped into *our* traditions. They can be important cords that bind the household together.

- *Spiritual life*. A final area that is sometimes a focus of tension between the generations is the spiritual dimension. If your parents and/or hers are not Christians, you know all too well that what's important to you is not always important to them, and vice versa. Your commitment of time and money to the church as well as your entire life style of serving may draw objections — anything from the silent treatment to open tirade.

However, anything you endure is probably mild compared to what happens in less tolerant cultures, where outraged parents, with the help of the law, can back up their religious preferences with violence. Jesus warned us that at times his message might "turn 'a man against his father, a daughter against her mother, and a daughter-in-law against her mother-in-law. A man's enemies will be the members of his own household' " (Matt. 10:35,36).

But he continued with a strong statement about where our ultimate allegiance lies: "Anyone who loves his father or mother more than me is not worthy of me . . . and anyone who does not take his cross and follow me is not worthy of me" (vv. 37,38).

We know from experience that the faithful carrying of the cross in our daily lives can sometimes have a dramatic effect on non-Christian parents. The words that we say and, even more importantly, the lives that we live can be the means of spiritual awakening. The joy of seeing one's own parents surrender to Christ has to be one of life's greatest moments.

Some guidelines

As we thread our way through the above areas of potential conflict — and others like them that we haven't mentioned — here are some watchwords to pin to the front wall of our minds:

1. *The household is not for sale.* As much as we want to please our parents, we must not give up the identity or the integrity of God's gift to *us*, our homes. We must fulfill our mission; we must do and be what God has directed us to do and be, regardless. As Jesus said, "Haven't you read . . . 'For this reason a man will leave his father and mother and be united to his wife'? . . . Therefore what God has joined together, let man not separate" (Matt. 19:4–6).

Leaving our father and mother may mean geographical separation. It almost certainly means psychological detachment. Your household must never be in bondage — emotionally, financially, or any other way — to someone else in the clan.

But . . . let's temper this with a second guideline:

2. *Diplomacy is better than confrontation*. You know your parents pretty well, and by now you've discovered the right and wrong ways to resolve conflicts with them. You know what causes a major blow-up. You know what helps to defuse a situation. As often as possible, without compromising your integrity, you're wise to adjust and bend.

If your father-in-law feels like maligning your favorite senator over dinner, it won't kill you to keep still. If your mother persists in nagging you about taking care of your health as if you were still twelve years old — what difference does it make? Just smile, and keep moving.

People who have lived to their age are not likely to do a lot of changing in the remaining years. Any campaign of yours to improve them or change their basic values or habits is unlikely to get far. About the only thing you'll accomplish is to irritate the relationship between the two of you. So save your energy. Be a nice guy, huh?

Which brings us to number three:

3. *Keep your mouth shut about the sins of other people's relatives — especially your wife's*. Let her do the criticizing. If she feels like saying, "My mother is absolutely unreasonable," that's her business, but don't *you* say it, even if it's true. Yankees don't go to Arkansas and tell hillbilly jokes; they leave that to the Arkansans.

After all, most of us have the common courtesy not to make negative remarks about a family member of someone such as our boss or a colleague at work. Why should you sound off about your in-laws? No matter how perceptive your comments, they will raise your wife's defenses and serve no useful purpose. Even humor is likely to backfire in this case; mother-in-law jokes are usually troublemakers.

You and your wife may come to a point where you can talk openly about her family's weaknesses without tensing up. She may need to work through some of the hurts of the past by verbalizing them. Even so, wait for her to lead you throughout the conversation. Never go further than she has already gone. And keep looking for ways to balance her perspective, to help her remember the strong points as well as the problems.

Virtually every father-in-law has something a son-in-law can relate to and appreciate. Virtually every mother-in-law is good at something. The sooner we learn to relax with them, let our hair down, and enjoy the areas of common interest, the better for all concerned. We don't have to impress them any more. We're not back in the courting days. For better or worse, they're stuck with us, and we with them, and we all might as well enjoy it.

As the years go by, parents — both our wives' and our own — need more and more of our patience and understanding as they may become less and less able to care for themselves. In time, the relationship turns upside down as we find ourselves making many of their major decisions and "parenting" them through the final years. Many husbands and wives in our society aren't willing to be the servants of their parents when they get old and sick. It takes time and a great deal of wisdom.

The Scripture is clear that "if a widow has children or grandchildren, these should learn first of all to put their religion into practice by caring for their own family and so repaying their parents and grandparents, for this is pleasing to God" (1 Tim. 5:4). Some Christians seek to obey this verse by bringing the aged parent into their own homes, even though this means a major adjustment in the family life. Others provide institutional care — but are diligent at the same time to find ways to keep the parent alive mentally and spiritually, not just physically.

Eventually, each of us will experience the loss of our parents and parents-in-law. From that vantage point, their idiosyncrasies won't seem so important after all. What will stick in our memories, though, is the quality of the relationship that we maintained while they were with us. That quality deserves our attention now.

I know one young husband who recently adjusted his work responsibilities and moved his family from San Diego to the Seattle area essentially to be close to the grandparents. He and his wife considered it important enough for their two children to know and participate in the extended family that they made a 1,300-mile relocation.

The generation that gave us birth can contribute a great deal to the life of our households. Instead of tension and frustration, we can have the benefits of their maturity and wisdom in a healthy, mutually respectful relationship. It depends in part upon them. It also depends upon us.

13

The Big Picture

13

The Big Picture

Have you heard of the Fifth Spiritual Law?

5. God loves you and has a wonderful plan for your household.

With due apologies to the people who promulgated the first four, I'd like to suggest that God is indeed concerned with the overall development of the Invisible Province he's given us. He has called us to serve our wives and children day by day; he also has some things in mind for the long haul that deserve our attention.

The business world talks a lot about goal-setting, management by objective, five-year plans, career progress. Businessmen have to look to the future; they hire consultants and forecasters to help lay out projections; they listen to the witty and sometimes corny slogans of motivation experts urging us all to set our sights on brighter, preplanned tomorrows.

This push for *goals* sometimes becomes so strong that we forget about *process*, with some rather dehumanizing results. A company division not making a fat enough contribution to the corporate profit gets shut down, throwing several hundred people out of work and perhaps upsetting the life of an entire community. Bright prospects in another product line may cause executives to demand unreasonable overtime from their people.

So in our quieter moments, we know that goals ought not to be lord and master of our lives. They are important, but not all-important. We were created to *be* as well as to *do*, and neither ought to be allowed to overpower the other.

The magnificent thing about God's planning is that it is totally wise and good, and it never compromises personhood. Thus, when we turn to the future of our families, the question is not: What goals shall we set? It is: *What is God's will for our household?*

This is not meant as a pious dodge of responsibility. God's planning is more than just platitudinous; it comes down to specifics. If we're listening, we can hear his very specific input from time to time, especially when we find ourselves facing major decisions. For example, an opportunity comes to change jobs. What shall we do? If we make up our minds solely on the basis of which firm is offering the better financial package, we've short-circuited the whole process. What would a change mean to the household in terms of moving, of different working hours, of happiness and fulfillment in the job once the new wears off, and a number of other things?

Younger couples tend to face these decisions more frequently, simply because there are more low and middle-level positions in the job market to be filled. Over a year's time, any company is out looking for more trainees and assistant supervisors than vice-presidents. During our first few years of marriage Grace and I began noticing a pattern: it seemed like every spring we had one or more job offers to think through. It got to the place that when March would roll around, we'd say, "Well, I wonder what it'll be this year."

Job decisions are tough ones; in spite of all your research, you're almost always left with a stack of unknowns. Even the counsel of trusted advisors is sometimes conflicting. Thus it is crucial that you and your wife turn to the only source of omniscience, the God who has planned that this question come into your life in the first place. What is his will for your future?

The wisdom of his answer may not be immediately apparent. Only now do I see how the work experiences of my earlier years were pieces of a puzzle that together form the background for what I'm currently doing. God was in those moves, even though sometimes we wondered. His strategy has become apparent only with time.

Another major part of the will of God for the household has to do with children. To have or not to have? If to have, how many? When? Modern contraception has given us control over all these questions. How should we decide?

Most of our wives, of course, start from an entirely different point than we do. They have a vested interest; after all, their bodies are rather directly involved in the process! Furthermore, the society (and, some would say, biology as well) has programed them to want to be mothers. First there were years of playing with dolls; then more years of baby-sitting. As a result, it's not uncommon to find a wife considerably more psyched up for parenting than her husband.

There are exceptions, of course. More and more women today want to do a number of other things *along with* mothering. Some want to do their things *instead of* mothering. And some modern husbands think having six kids would be just great.

Once again we're faced with a complex question. We

can debate the wisdom of Zero Population Growth. We can analyze the decline of the birth rate in the United States from 3.76 children per woman to 1.75 in just the last twenty years. We can count the financial cost. Indeed, we ought to examine our own motives: are we hesitating simply because we don't want to be bothered? Is it a matter of not wanting to serve another human life in the household? Face it: parenting is primarily an experience of giving, not getting. There are rewards, but there's a lot more that's mostly serving.

God calls us and our wives to think deeply about these things and to discuss them as long as necessary. They have tremendous import; the decision to have a child or not has ramifications for years to come. Some couples give more thought to the purchase of new stereo components than they do to starting or enlarging a family. It is imperative that we make time for prayer and meditation until we are sure we have the mind of Christ. We dare not plan by default.

The tough decisions never stop coming. How shall a child be educated? Is it more important that he get the spiritual nurturing of a Christian school? But shouldn't Christians be the salt of the earth; if we abandon the public school system, are we neglecting a potential influence in the community?

What about long-range financial priorities? Can we handle this big a mortgage? How much insurance do we really need? If we trade cars now, will the next couple of years be a constant squeeze? The motto of America is buy now, pay later; one man in Los Altos, California, has been able to accumulate over eight hundred credit cards in his own name as a hobby. There's no shortage of credit for most of us, but there's a dire shortage of sense in knowing how to use — or refuse — it. And often only God can give us the fortitude to say no to a tempting expenditure or investment that, in the long run, is not the best for the household. Again, it comes down to whether we ask for his input.

Should I go back to school? Should she go back to school? Should I run for a public office? Should she? In all of these areas, and others like them, God reveals the big picture as we wait before him. He reveals it to us husbands, since we are the ones whom he has designated the head of the household. He reveals it to us and our wives together, since we are joint recipients of his gifts. And God may reveal his plan to the wife alone if her husband isn't listening to the divine voice. God is possibly less concerned than we are with the routing of his communication; what he desperately wants is for us to have the benefit of his wisdom. But we, the leader/servants of the household, should be the most eager to receive it.

God made an interesting comment about one husband in Genesis 18:19 — "I have chosen him, that he may charge his children and his household after him to keep the way of the Lord by doing righteousness and justice; so that the Lord may bring to Abraham what he has promised him." Abraham was apparently a pacesetter in his home. He established "the way of the Lord" as the family pattern. And that diligence at home, where few others could see, apparently unleashed the remarkable public aspects of God's plan for his household throughout his life and even after he was gone.

I believe God has great things in mind for my household and yours. We must not block their coming. We must be what God has called us to be, do what he has asked us to do, serve where he has placed us to serve — and watch what happens. The apostle Paul was "confident of this, that he who began a good work in you will carry it on to completion" (Phil. 1:6). We are all on the way. We're not yet the husbands God wants to make us. But we're coming along.

"Finally, brothers, whatever is true, whatever is noble, whatever is right. . . . Whatever you have learned or received or heard . . . put it into practice. And the God of peace will be with you" (Phil. 4:8,9).